The Science of *Being Lucky*:
How to Engineer Good Fortune, Consistently Catch Lucky Breaks, and Live a Charmed Life

by Nick Trenton
www.NickTrenton.com

Table of Contents

INTRODUCTION	**7**
LSD's Discovery	11
Why luck matters	16
Luck or hard work?	20
CHAPTER 1. LUCK OF THE DRAW	**27**
The Human Need for Control	29
The "Scientific" View on Luck	33
Locus of Control	36
Stable vs. Fleeting Luck	46
Attribution Theory	50
CHAPTER 2. WHAT TO BELIEVE	**57**
The Law of Attraction	59
The Self-Fulfilling Prophecy	69
The Power of Belief	73
CHAPTER 3. WHAT TO THINK	**81**
Lucky Traits	83
Lucky thought patterns	95
CHAPTER 4. WHAT TO DO	**107**
Task 1: Work harder	108
Task 2: Use the Luck Surface Area Theory	111
Task 3: Visualize and Repeat Affirmations	122
What about superstitions?	130

CHAPTER 5. COINCIDENCE AND SERENDIPITY — 141

THE "SERENDIPITY MINDSET" — 143
SERENDIPITY — 153
COINCIDENCE — 158

CHAPTER 6. WISEMAN'S FOUR FACTORS — 171

BE OPEN TO NEW EXPERIENCES — 174
LISTEN TO YOUR GUT — 176
POSITIVE EXPECTATIONS — 179
TRANSFORM BAD LUCK INTO GOOD — 181
HOW TO STRENGTHEN THE FOUR FACTORS — 184

CHAPTER 7. "STRATEGIC LUCK PLANNING" — 199

SUMMARY GUIDE — 227

Introduction

I wish I could say this story happened to a friend, but alas, it happened to me.

If you've never been to Las Vegas, there are actually not that many things to do, in my opinion. Correction – there are many things to do, but they all fall into a few general categories. If you're into the nightlife, the scene there is unparalleled. But if you're not, like me, then mostly what there is to do is spend too much money on extravagant activities or simply lose it gambling.

I chose to engage in the latter. This was during my third trip there, so I considered myself experienced in the nuances of gambling and superstitions. After all, I had won roughly $200 on my last trip to the roulette table, so I felt like I knew what I was doing.

Now, this isn't a story about me losing a fortune. Instead, it's a story about my naked lack of understanding about how some people treat the concept of good luck and attempt to bend the will of the universe to suit their needs. *So there I was*, back at the roulette table with my lucky penny in my pocket, when I sit down next to a man who smelled like a dirty laundry hamper, and that's putting it mildly.

He was dressed in a suit, and his hair looked clean and non-greasy. So, what was happening here? What odd situation did I find myself in at this roulette table? I must have made some sort of face in reaction to the smell, because the man apologetically smiled and told me that he was sorry for the smell, and that it was attributable to his lucky socks. He pulled up his pant legs and showed me a pair of ratty, beige socks riddled with holes, and which didn't appear to have any elastic left in them. The socks probably started as white but became beige through years of wear and lack of washing.

Before placing our bets, the man sheepishly grinned and said, "Last washed eight years ago. Gotta keep that luck juice!"

At that moment, I suddenly knew that my good luck charms and rituals paled compared to what was happening in the world. I left shortly thereafter.

The Science of Being Lucky — good luck, being lucky, and avoiding bad luck — examines humanity's curious tendency to want to feel included in what their life has in store for them. Think about it this way: Is it more comforting to have a steering wheel appear to change the car's direction, or have no steering wheel at all and suddenly you are headed straight at a wall?

Call it fate, or "being in the right place at the right time," we all have our pet theories about possible cheat codes for the universe, and how to win whatever game it is we're playing – big or small. And we all want to avoid that sinking feeling that we've somehow taken a wrong step or caused a potential lucky break to slip through our fingers. Whatever luck is, we want it on our side. It seemingly has the ability to create the life we want, or leave us in ruins. If we're in the right place at the right time, perhaps we'll run into that one person who can make a huge difference in our career. Haven't all the celebrities and entrepreneurs told that story?

Is luck just another word for cosmic fate that we are born with, or is it something that is manipulated by good luck charms like unwashed socks or avoiding black cats? To put it more succinctly, is there a certain way we can act, in practical terms, that will make us more susceptible to better outcomes, and what we might consider better luck? Some people would find the very question preposterous – and then secretly wonder what the answer is.

Luckily, the results are in, and it's been proven that luck *is* a trait that can be engineered and manufactured. It has nothing to do with four leaf clovers or broken mirrors and everything to do with changing the way we imagine the concept of luck. Thankfully, it's got nothing to do with "luck juice" and unwashed socks!

Is this book going to help you become luckier and lead what appears to be a semi-charmed life? If you mean that it will lead you to more beneficial situations in every walk of life, then yes. After all, that's what we're really after with luck, isn't it?

LSD's Discovery

There are many instances of luck in the field of science, from the notion that an apple fell onto Isaac Newton's head, prompting him to investigate the concept of gravity, to the invention of Viagra, which was originally supposed to be a heart medication.

The case study I want to focus on is the development and subsequent discovery of *lysergic acid diethylamide*, otherwise known as the psychedelic drug LSD. The discovery of LSD may be of dubious utility to most, but the point is that it demonstrates a path that took extreme openness and curiosity to fulfill.

Albert Hoffman discovered LSD in 1943, but it was the result of years of a zig-zag path that began with the intent to create a medical compound to combat ergot, a fungus that was responsible for thousands of deaths as a result of tainted food stores. In the year 857, ergot was theorized to be responsible for an immense plague that came to be known as St. Anthony's Fire. Needless to say, decades of research against the effects of ergot had been conducted — how to reduce it, neutralize it, and deal with the ensuing symptoms.

Hoffman was originally piggybacking on the work of fellow researcher Arthur Stoll's initiatives, whose biggest accomplishment was to break down ergot into two distinct compounds: ergotamine and ergobasine. Following this research, Hoffman experimented with lysergic acid and ergot, eventually producing a compound he called LSD-25. As with any new compound, it was tested for medical properties, and there were none apparent except "*the experimental animals became restless during the narcosis.*" Ultimately, the researchers went on to say, "The new substance, however, aroused no special interest in our pharmacologists and physicians; testing was therefore discontinued."

After LSD-25 sat in the dark for roughly five years, Hoffman admitted that he never forgot about it and had always had a certain fixation and curiosity about it. He always remembered the way those animals reacted when exposed to it, and thought there was something special on his hands. This led to Hoffman creating LSD-25 again in 1943 and conducting experiments on it.

However, his experiments and trials did not go exactly to plan. In fact, he became his first test subject inadvertently. One day while at work in his lab with close exposure to the substance, he suddenly felt so mentally uncomfortable that he had to go home for the day.

Here's what he wrote in his diary about the experience:

"I was forced to interrupt my work in the laboratory in the middle of the afternoon and proceed home, being affected by a remarkable restlessness, combined with a slight dizziness. At home, I lay down and sank into a not unpleasant intoxicated-like condition, characterized by an extremely stimulated imagination. In a dream-like state, with eyes closed (I found the daylight to be unpleasantly glaring), I perceived an uninterrupted steam of fantastic pictures, extraordinary shapes with intense, kaleidoscopic play of colors."

When he returned to work, he naturally attempted to discover what had caused such an odd reaction. It must have been something in the lab, and he concluded he had likely ingested a small amount of LSD-25, likely through his fingertips. For such a small amount to cause such a massive reaction was startling, and he decided to engage in further self-experimentation to investigate the symptoms further.

Now that his intuition about LSD was showing tantalizing signs of proving justified, Hofmann decided there was only one course of action: self-experimentation. He later wrote more about his fortuitous afternoon exposure to LSD-25:

"Here the notes in my laboratory journal cease. I was able to write the last words only with great effort. By now it was already clear to me that LSD had been the cause of the remarkable experience of the previous Friday, for the altered perceptions were of the same type as before, only much more intense. I had to struggle to speak intelligibly. I asked my laboratory assistant, who was informed of the self-experiment, to escort me home. We went by bicycle, no automobile being available because of wartime restrictions on their use. On the way home, my condition began to assume threatening forms. Everything in my field of vision wavered and was distorted as if seen in a curved mirror. I also had the sensation of being unable to move from the spot. Nevertheless, my assistant later told me that we had traveled very rapidly. Finally, we arrived at home safe and sound, and I was just barely capable of

asking my companion to summon our family doctor and request milk from the neighbors.

The dizziness and sensation of fainting became so strong at times that I could no longer hold myself erect, and had to lie down on a sofa. My surroundings had now transformed themselves in more terrifying ways. Everything in the room spun around, and the familiar objects and pieces of furniture assumed grotesque, threatening forms. They were in continuous motion, animated, as if driven by an inner restlessness. The lady next door, whom I scarcely recognized, brought me milk — in the course of the evening I drank more than two liters. She was no longer Mrs. R., but rather a malevolent, insidious witch with a colored mask."

Hoffman began testing the substance on animals, and he noted that animals had curious reactions similar to his. Mice began moving and walking oddly and licking everything in sight. Cats appeared to be anxious but with immense amounts of salivation. Chimpanzees were not perceptibly affected by the researchers, but other chimpanzees around the drugged chimpanzees became upset and disgusted, so the drugged chimpanzees were obviously acting in a way extremely foreign to their social norms.

And of course, LSD usage in humans results in similar symptoms. There's a reason is it a noted psychedelic that has been reported to produce hallucinations, voices, and feelings of euphoria.

So how does the curious case of LSD exemplify the presence of luck in scientific discovery? Hoffman approached LSD in a way that all but guaranteed a lucky discovery.

Why luck matters

We tend to think of luck as something rare and unexpected, but what if it plays a predictable and recurring role in what we call success? We believe that personal characteristics like talent, hard work, resilience and so on are responsible for people's success – and to some degree, they are. But there is always an extra element that seemingly isn't explained by personal attributes. Author and risk analyst Nassim Taleb and economist Robert Frank believe that luck plays a bigger role than we think – that luck, in fact, is everything.

That businessman who is crediting his fortune to hustle skills and a growth mindset? Well, research by Branko Milanovic at the World Bank School of Public Policy found that 50% of the variability in people's income can be explained by the country in which they were born, and how income is distributed in that country. A paper in The Journal of Economic Perspectives by Liran Einav and Leeat Yariv showed that people with last names beginning with letters higher in the alphabet were more likely to receive tenure, which must have made for interesting reading for their supervisors. Meanwhile, a 2009 working paper by Bentley Coffey & Patrick McLaughlin suggests that women with masculine sounding names are more successful in legal careers.

The hidden dimension of "luck", which seems to invisibly influence our opportunities and successes, is arguably a mix of political, social and economic mechanisms of which we only see the end results – and assume randomness. Maybe, the most "successful" people in the world really are just the luckiest. Or, they're the people who've learned the rules of that hidden dimension.

Alessandro Pluchino, Andrea Raspirarda and Alessio Biondo weren't content just asking this question theoretically – they built a toy mathematical model to actually quantify this thing we call luck. The model simulated the careers of a population over 40 years. All the hypothetical people were given varying degrees of talent but the same degree of success to start. The model was run and assessed at intervals, with a "lucky event" occurring every 6 months. The results? They found that encountering a lucky event doubled success *in proportion to one's talent*, and that a small number of people always ended up with the bulk of the success in any population. So, while talent was normally distributed, success was always drastically skewed. In our world, just eight men possess the wealth of the billions of people in the poorest half of the human population, so the model appears to replicate reality!

From the paper Pluchino, Raspirarda and Alessio published:

> "It is very well known that intelligence (or, more in general, *talent* and personal qualities) exhibits a Gaussian distribution among the population, whereas the distribution of wealth —

often considered as a proxy of success — follows typically a power law (Pareto law), with a large majority of poor people and a very small number of billionaires. Such a discrepancy between a Normal distribution of inputs, with a typical scale (the average talent or intelligence), and the scale-invariant distribution of outputs, suggests that some hidden ingredient is at work behind the scenes. In this paper, we suggest that such an ingredient is just randomness. In particular, our simple agent-based model shows that, if it is true that some degree of talent is necessary to be successful in life, almost never the most talented people reach the highest peaks of success, being overtaken by averagely talented but sensibly luckier individuals."

The biggest finding? Initial talent did not predict success. In fact, it had nothing to do with it. Talent allowed people to exploit opportunities that emerged by luck, but talent alone was insufficient. In other words, mediocre but lucky won out over talented but unlucky. If you've ever read a celebrity magazine, this comes as no surprise...

The results of this study have spurred interesting questions around meritocracy and how to build our society to make the best use of real talent and potential. The authors are especially interested in how funding can change the luck landscape and tip the scales. But what should *we* make of the findings? In the following chapters, we'll be exploring how to maximize our chances of a "lucky event" and how to leverage the hidden rules and laws governing the distribution of this luck. If the secret ingredient is randomness, is there a way to invite more of it into our lives? If improving your raw talent and merit is not what results in success, then what does? For now, it's enough to note that luck is not merely something nice to have on top of a sound strategy for success – it is basically the *only* strategy!

Luck or hard work?

Warren Buffett, easily considered one of the world's most successful individuals, understands the role of luck. He calls it the "Ovarian Lottery." Whether you are born male or female, in America or Afghanistan, to rich or poor parents, "it's the most important thing that's ever going to happen to you in your life. It's going to determine way more than what school you go to, how hard you work, all kinds of things."

But what about Croatian man Frano Selak? He's been called both the luckiest and unluckiest man in the world, with an astonishing number of near-death experiences. First, he was rescued from a train wreck when 17 others died. On the only plane trip he took, he was blown out of a malfunctioning hatch… only to land on a haystack and survive. The plane crashed, and 19 people died. He survived a bus crash that killed four with only minor scrapes. He survived not one but two car crashes. Shortly after his 73rd birthday, he won the equivalent of a million dollars in the lottery. It's hard to look at Selak's story and see anything but luck – surely he wasn't *responsible* for any of this?

Let's consider a completely different story. In 1969, Chinese scientist Tu Youyou was made head of a research group to create antimalarial medication to assist Vietnamese soldiers who were dying in the war. Youyou's team conducted extensive research, narrowing down thousands of potential remedies and painstakingly testing each one. Investigating the promising but inconsistent results from a kind of sweet wormwood, she happened upon a single sentence in a 1500-year-old Chinese text called *The Handbook of Prescriptions for Emergencies*. It was then that she realized she needed to redesign all her experiments, taking into account heat during the extraction of the plant.

In no time, the team had synthesized an effective antimalarial drug.
Youyou faced obstacle after obstacle in her research, but she pushed on, even infecting herself with malaria – and curing it – at a time she was prevented from conducting trials. It was a decade later when her work was finally released. Today, the drug has been administered more than a billion times, and has saved the lives of millions. Youyou

received the Nobel prize and a host of other awards.

But she had started without a postgrad degree, without research experience, and without being a member of any academies. She was diligent, hardworking and methodical. Was her success down to luck or hard work? And what makes her story different from Frano Selak's? The answer is that luck *and* hard work play a role, each interacting in interesting ways.

Luck may be more relevant in an **absolute sense**, while hard work matters in a **relative sense**. To explain: luck can bestow the right genes, good timing and beneficial connections, which can set you apart from others. This is like winning the lottery. But hard work distinguishes you from those who have the same amount of luck as you. How do you compare with other lottery winners?

It's pure luck to be born in a rich country, but hard work will determine how you compare to others who were also blessed with that fortune. The larger and more extravagant the success, the more likely it was luck! In other words, being a good musician is down to hard work, but being the biggest rock star of the decade is likely sheer luck. Taleb summarizes this by saying, "Mild success can be explainable by skills and labor. Wild success is attributable to variance."

So, again we see that it's not hard work OR luck, but a bit of both, depending on the scale of success we're talking about. It would be wrong to assume that winning the genetic lottery was a result of your personal efforts. Still, at the same time, if you're from a family of athletically gifted people, but only you found success as an athlete, that is probably because of your hard work.

Another way of thinking of it is to imagine that hard work determines the shape of our success trajectory in life, but we are all embarking from different starting points (luck). It is possible to overcome bad luck, and it's possible to lose any head start you were blessed with.

Luck is out of our control, yes. But we can learn to understand it and work with it, and optimize on the fortune that does come our way. Luck, as they say, is what happens when opportunity meets preparation. We *can* control our effort, essentially increasing our "luck surface area" and making it so that when a lucky break flies along, we're in the best position to catch it.

Takeaways:

- Luck may play a bigger role in our success than we think. By examining what we consider lucky breaks, serendipity and fortuitous events, we can better handle the invisible forces that favor some and not others.
- Research has made surprising findings, i.e., that it may be better to be mediocre in skills but lucky than to be highly talented yet unlucky. Mathematical models have tended to show the irrelevance of skill and talent, and emphasize the fact that randomness plays a big part in what we consider success.
- In the case of the discovery of LSD (and many other scientific advances), we can see that luck plays a surprising role.
- Luck may play a role in an absolute sense in determining the hand we're dealt in what Warren Buffett calls the "Ovarian Lottery" – where we're born, our genes, and so on. But hard work does matter, and may factor in a more relative sense, i.e., it helps us distinguish ourselves from others who have been similarly lucky.

- Luck and hard work play a part. We cannot control luck, but we can understand how it works and position ourselves accordingly, so that we're ready to strike when and if opportunity does come our way.

Chapter 1. Luck of the Draw

So much for some of the research into the area, but let's take a closer look. What is luck more generally, and why do people want it so badly? Why do we even care if black cats cross our paths, or if we are wearing our smelly yet lucky underwear while watching our favorite teams play?

We all grow up with the general idea that our actions are not the only factor at play in the outcomes of our lives — that there is some amount of random chance that's either working in our favor or against it. We call this random chance *luck*. If we're *lucky*, good things happen, and if we're *unlucky*, bad things happen.

The belief in luck has manifested itself in different ways for different cultures and traditions for as long as there has been recorded history. In Western countries, there's an old saying: "See a penny, pick it up, and all day long you'll have good luck." In Eastern countries, you often can't enter a restaurant without catching a glimpse of a statue of a cat waving at you.

Whatever the case, the idea of having good fortune and doing everything possible to channel this ephemeral blessing is often far more valuable to people than the coins or cats themselves. It may work, and it may not – but in the off-chance it does, it can't hurt, right? Just as accumulating good luck is highly desirable, avoiding bad luck is also of significant importance in many cultures. In fact, there are countless superstitions people hold for the sole purpose of avoiding misfortune, such as skipping the 13th floor in high-rise buildings or not walking under ladders. You may have your own personal superstitions about how to avert disaster.

In either case, the thing about lucky charms and superstitions is that they represent our human attempt to control what seems uncontrollable. These forces were ascribed to the fates or malevolent spirits in the past. Today, the idea that things happen "for no reason" or because of random chance is no less terrifying – and we still try to appease those gods of chaos and randomness, if we can.

The only thing we know for sure about luck is that we want to have it on our side.

The Human Need for Control

We have developed an increasingly better understanding of our world and universe throughout history. Yet even now, many of the complexities of our day-to-day existence are so far beyond comprehension that we can only reliably predict and understand a tiny fraction of them. It doesn't matter if you're one of the world's top engineers — there are still things that would appear magical to you. We know logically that everything is a result of cause and effect. Still, when we are unable to actually see the underlying cause and effect in a given scenario, we have a strong tendency to find or create other explanations for why everything is the way it is. This is an unavoidably human emotional reaction to the sometimes vast and ungraspable laws of the natural world. The idea of luck is one way we understand these complex universal mechanisms. In the face of randomness, we can still get to feel somewhat in control and less subject to the realities of chaos theory.

We are constantly seeking control, so we think if we could only know what is going to happen, then we would be able to use that knowledge to our advantage. It's arguable this is the very foundation of the scientific method itself! Good luck charms, superstitions and rituals, then, can be seen to come from the same impulse, although nobody would call them scientific.

This drive for control causes us to model, predict, and manage the world around us, which has led to a great deal of scientific and technological advancement over time — but it also comes at a cost. Where we find limited or no success in our ability to understand our surroundings, we *lie* to ourselves to fill in the gaps. When things don't go as we planned or hoped, we simply explain away our failures as resulting from the incompetence of others, or just plain bad luck. "Bad luck" becomes a black box, or a container into which we can file away all the unexplained, unaccountable events we frustratingly lack an explanation for.

A blackjack player can control their bet and whether they hit or stay, but to beat the house consistently enough to win some money, they'll need random chance to go in their favor more often than it goes against them. They'll need luck. The act of counting cards is important to explore here: does remembering the cards that have already been used from a deck and using that data to calculate probabilities of success given the composition of remaining cards, card counters can make better-informed decisions at the blackjack table. They make that black box smaller and give luck less chance to act.

Is it still "lucky" to win at gambling if you know the probabilities for all the cards being dealt? At what point does luck turn into an informed decision or calculated risk based on statistics?

And luck doesn't just apply to good things happening to us; it also applies to narrowly *avoiding* bad things happening to us — instances when the danger or negative consequences were close enough to feel. For example, someone may consider themselves lucky to be alive after escaping a car crash relatively unscathed. It would be fairly jarring to realize that you could have died, and no amount of luck or lucky underwear would have saved you — it's just how random and chaotic the world can be. As you are sitting right now and reading this sentence, who is to say there haven't already been countless unseen events that have spared your life – without you even realizing it's happened?

Things are continuously happening to us and around us, and we often have no ability to intervene or otherwise impact the outcomes of events in our own lives. Our winning days at the casino and the near-misses driving on the interstate are due to good fortune, while the losing days and when actual harm does come to us result from bad luck.

Luck, then, is simply an *explanation* for why good and bad things happen to us; an attribute we use to give meaning to random events. It's the story we tell to give us the illusion of understanding – and by extension, control.

The idea of luck is not only useful for making ourselves feel better about the chaos around us. We also commonly use luck to make others feel better, too, attributing our own successes to luck rather than skill to make another person feel okay about their failures. When a basketball player makes a half-court shot at the last second to win a game, it will likely be called a "lucky shot" whether the player practices half-court shots consistently or not. The other team might still feel bad about their loss, but knowing they just caught an unlucky break can alleviate their sense of responsibility for coming up short. "Bad luck" can also explain away poor performances, protecting not just our egos but our very sense of justice and the way the world works.

These examples illustrate how we tend to use luck as an attribution to create false meaning in the effort to make ourselves and others feel better. Ultimately, what we can realize is that luck is not something that comes from the gods or nature. It is a human creation — *a coping mechanism* — for explaining that which we can't logically or rationally explain ourselves.

The "Scientific" View on Luck

Given what we now know about luck, you may not be surprised that the concept of luck is regularly at odds with a scientific understanding of the world. And in fact, scientists often describe what we call luck by another name — chance and probability.

Upon closer examination, this simple change in terminology can be uncomfortable for many people. This is because even though luck itself may not be within our control, it does at least give us a feeling of control over a world governed by random chance. We may unconsciously imagine that luck is still doled out according to merit somehow, or according to the dictates of "fate." And believing in luck can potentially be even more comforting for many people if that belief coincides with the idea that there's always the chance to get more luck.

Nobel Prize winner and Princeton math professor John Nash is quoted in the movie *A Beautiful Mind,* saying, "I don't believe in luck, but I do believe in assigning a value to things." We can infer that the "value" John Nash is referring to is a probability that in a random scenario given the circumstances "A," the outcome will be "B," "C," or "D." Through this scientific approach, we can't predict exactly what will happen, but we can model the likelihood of each of the possible outcomes based on the information we do have.

Luck is entirely absent from this equation, replaced by chance in the form of probabilities.

To an outsider who doesn't understand or consider the probabilities of each outcome, they may consider themselves lucky if their most desirable outcomes become a reality, and unlucky if not. But if the outcomes they desire are statically improbable, and in the end, they don't occur, is there actually anything unlucky about that? A scientist would more than likely argue not. They would suggest that "luck" in this case is a human intervention alone. It's not personal. The outcomes didn't really happen *to* anyone – they just happened. After all, is a single event that favors one and punishes another a lucky or unlucky one? What happens if we remove the human interpretation completely?

Brad Watson, scientist and author of the booklet, *There Are No Coincidences — there is synchronism, design and alignment,* said that Nash was both wrong and right. Watson believes that luck is an integral part of our existence, and even went so far as to create an equation that assigns a value to luck:

Luck 100 =
[karma 4 + modesty 1] x
[desire 4 + actions 4 + abilities 4 +
contribution 4 + blessings 4]

Watson leaves it up to the individual to interpret this equation, and your own feelings about luck may determine what, if anything, it means to you. Again, we see that luck always seems to be colored with inescapable narrative elements. However, one need only examine some of Watson's other beliefs — such as the one that he is the reincarnation of both Jesus and Albert Einstein — to get an idea of how luck and deception often go hand in hand.

Locus of Control

In the field of personality psychology, the locus of control is defined as the strength of a person's belief that they — and not external forces beyond their control — determine the experiences and outcomes of their own life. This is important: it suggests that the phenomenon of luck and our *human perception of* that luck are two different things. Again, we are dealing with attributions made by human beings with a particular stake in random, impersonal events.

Jean-Paul Sartre and Sigmund Freud are two among many philosophers and psychologists who have attributed a belief in luck to a *lower* degree locus of control for one's life, and subsequently, an outlet for escape from personal responsibility. Believing in luck is comforting when we fail or otherwise feel dissatisfied, because the blame for all of the negative consequences can be shifted away from us. In this case, we didn't need to work harder or take a different approach; all we needed was a little more good luck, and we could have been successful.

With an external locus of control, you dial down your own agency and see the events of your life as outside of your influence. With an internal locus of control, you see yourself as the main driver of events. Psychologists are interested in this attribution of events and want to see how functional it is, i.e., which mindset is most likely to lead to wellbeing and success. Unlike statisticians or philosophers, however, they have little to say about the objective accuracy of these attitudes – perceptions aside, how much *do* humans have control over the outcomes of their lives?

I would be remiss in mentioning the concept of control over luck without talking about the **Gambler's Fallacy**. The Gambler's Fallacy is the feeling that there are predictable patterns in what are actually random sets of events. Here's a question: if you flip a coin and ten

times in a row the coin lands face up, what is the probability
that the next flip will reveal tails?

The correct answer is that the probability is 50%. It is *always* 50%. But for the human onlooker, the more heads that appear, the more overdue are the tails, and the more likely they are to bet money that the next flip will be tails. Statisticians have long known that the mathematical laws of probability are seldom in alignment with what our human, story-making minds think should happen, i.e., what we feel is "intuitive."

For example, if you roll dice, you might feel that you should eventually roll a seven because… it's just time for it to happen. Never mind the fact that this is not statistically or probabilistically sound; you are attempting to create order in something impossible to have control over. You want to manipulate a quantity that will supposedly change the outcome: luck.

You are also attempting to find logic and an explanation for a random series of events. There is no better illustration than how early mankind started to see entire scenes in the night sky in the form of constellations. The pattern of stars in the sky are certainly randomized, but humans tend to find patterns and put things into contexts we already know. While such an ability was and is crucial for our survival in the world, it makes us bad at understanding probability. Really bad.

The Gambler's Fallacy is the notion that just because X happened, Y should happen, X shouldn't happen, or X should happen again. More often than not, these events are all independent of each other, which should guide your decision-making to be less biased. Humans have a bias towards narrative, and are looking for cause and effect relationships (or even, if you like, punishment and reward) where it may not exist.

This cognitive bias represents a broader phenomenon known as apophenia, which is the human tendency to see patterns and connections in random data points. This is why people see rabbits in clouds and elaborate scenes in inkblot tests. The term was coined by neurologist Klaus Conrad, who defined the tendency as an "unmotivated seeing of connections." It seems to stem from an evolutionary desire to make sense of information and understand the current environment we are in.

Apophenia likely did serve an important purpose for those who constantly had to think about their safety and security. This still applies to many of us who live outside the concrete jungles of cities and towns. If you recognize a pattern of danger, you can more easily flee, fight back, and survive. If you miss these patterns, you're going to be something's dinner. One's propensity for apophenia could literally mean the difference between life and death. For instance, you might notice leaves rustling, the birds have disappeared, and dust is rising from a nearby bush. If you fail to put together that this is a pattern of an impending attack from a jaguar, then you're dinner. It turns out seeing patterns where they may not exist can be a boon — though not when you are gambling. However, they can also lead to a skewed perception of reality.

Apophenia, notably, gives rise to the locus of control.

Renowned psychologist Julian Rotter first developed the principle of locus of control in 1954. The main consideration of his theory is people's belief that control either resides internally or externally — within yourself, or within others and external circumstances.

Whether you can truly control your reality, or if it is purely subject to others.

In 1990, Rotter described the internal locus of control as "the degree to which persons expect that a reinforcement or an outcome of their behavior is contingent on their own behavior or personal characteristics." Such an expectation can have numerous benefits, including confidence and motivation to seek out information and develop skills that will enable them to better influence people and situations. This belief in their own control can also incentivize people with an internal locus of control to be highly success-oriented or become politically active. It makes sense: believing that your actions have a predictable and quantifiable effect on the world makes you more likely to take those actions.

On the other hand, Rotter described the external locus of control as "the degree to which persons expect that the reinforcement or outcome is a function of chance, luck, or fate, is under the control of powerful others, or is simply unpredictable." This fatalistic way of viewing the world does not come without its own benefits, including generally being more passive and accepting. If a person believes that they do not have any control over a given matter and should just be at peace with whatever happens, that can give them a very even-tempered approach to life. Or make them shrug and give up.

In sum, a person with a strong internal locus of control will take responsibility for the failure and success of their actions in achieving their desired outcome, believing that their failures are due to a lack of ability, focus, or effort. Meanwhile, a person with a mostly external locus of control will be likely to attribute their successes and failures to either being lucky or unlucky. Like many other personality traits, the locus of control is not merely black and white, but rather a spectrum. Some people have an entirely internal or external locus of control, but it is more common for individuals to have a mix of both of the views.

Interestingly, it is possible for an individual's position on the locus of control spectrum to change over the course of their life, in response to different events. While some people's outlook might be relatively static, the general trend is for younger and elderly people to have a higher external locus of control than middle-aged people who are more success-oriented during their career prime.

Due to their beliefs in their own self-control and ability to influence their environments, people with a high internal locus of control see their future as being in their own hands. In the case of children or the elderly, though, there may be objective limitations to what is and isn't in their scope of control.

There is, of course, a downside to high levels of personal responsibility. When failures inevitably occur, people with an internal locus of control may be tempted to accept the blame, rather than excusing the failure based on other people or circumstances.

On the contrary, people who have a high external locus of control believe that they have little or no control over events and what other people do. Some may even allow this lack of control to go even further, believing that other people actually have control over them and there is nothing that they can do besides fall in line and accept their fate.

So, how does luck figure into the locus of control? Well, guess who tends to possess a greater belief and even reliance upon the concept of luck? Those with an external locus of control — luck fits neatly into that description. Both luck and an external locus of control can be characterized by accepting what happens and relying on external events, even and especially those events you don't understand or even like.

When an individual possessing a high external locus of control finds success in life, they will be more likely to express modesty, attributing their successes to luck rather than their own skill and effort. It's not false humility — they believe it could have happened to anyone, and they were just lucky to be there. On the other hand, when they experience failure, they won't feel personally responsible to the same extent as a person with a high internal locus of control. They are able to conveniently blame bad luck, so they are less likely to dwell on failure for long.

Another characteristic of having an external locus of control is the relatively lower likelihood of being proactive or acting in their best interests. At its worst, this can look like apathy or a victim complex. When events are chaotic and complicated, they may take a step back and let things work themselves out, assuming that they wouldn't be able to make a significant difference anyway, even if they tried. As you can imagine, this isn't something that creates enormous feelings of competence or confidence.

Those with internal loci of control will beat themselves up when they fail (it is their fault, right?), but they're also more likely to take credit when they succeed, allowing it to boost their confidence in themselves – rightly or wrongly.

Someone with an external locus of control would be happy if you told them "good luck," whereas someone with an internal locus of control would reply, "I don't need luck!" Which are *you* more likely to say? That will likely tell you all you need to know about your locus of control and how you feel you contribute to your life's path. The more control you feel, the more responsible and accountable you feel, and thus the harder you work.

The big question here is, does our perception of luck actually impact the experience of luck in our lives? Whether we are accurate or inaccurate in our attributions and interpretations, is there an attitude most correlated with actual success?

Stable vs. Fleeting Luck

Researchers from UCLA and Columbia University teamed up to take a deeper look at how people's perceptions of luck vary and its impact on their behavior.

They found that generally, people who have an external locus of control can be broken up into two subcategories: those who believe luck is stable, and those who view it as fleeting.

Having a stable view of luck means that you believe people are consistently either lucky or unlucky — almost as if luck itself isn't so much an external force but rather a personality trait. If Michael wins at blackjack five trips to the casino in a row, he must be a really lucky guy. Forever.

The group that views luck as fleeting sees it as entirely external, believing that a person's luck is unpredictable and oscillates back and forth between favorable and unfavorable. Michael has been consistently lucky to win money five times in a row at the casino, so his luck is due to run out any day now. It was his "lucky day", but anything could happen tomorrow.

How do these views affect people personally?

For those individuals who have an external locus of control and a view that luck is stable, research has shown that this leads to a *higher* drive for achieving personal success. This stable outlook is correlated with greater feelings of personal control, which is in turn attributable to being more motivated and proactive about achieving the outcomes they desire.

This may seem surprising, but this phenomenon makes sense upon closer examination. If you believe in luck as a stable force, and you also believe that your personal luck is within your sphere of influence, it follows that you would be more *consistent* in pursuing your goals. We're dealing with luck, but a stable, known quantity of luck. After all, you have a fixed and knowable advantage over all those people who aren't as lucky as you.

On the contrary, taking the approach to luck as a random and un-influenceable can make you wonder, "What's the point of even trying?" You may as well live in a world where every outcome of every moment is determined by the random spin of a wheel. Even if something good happens in such a universe, all you can assume is that it is currently happening – nothing suggests that it will continue. But being skeptical and simply resigning yourself to your fate will undermine any motivation to make the effort to be successful in the first place.

Let's take an example from the restaurant industry. There are many myths about how many restaurants fail in the first few years after opening. Still, even conservative estimates put this number somewhere around 60% of restaurants failing within three years. We can imagine that somebody with an external locus of control and a fleeting view on luck might look at that probability for failure and say, "Why even bother? My restaurant would probably fail, anyway." Even if they had already made a success of a restaurant in the past, this would mean nothing. The random and often cruel hands of fate might just as easily smash their dreams of a subsequent restaurant.

Retain the same external locus of control, but switch the view on luck from fleeting to stable, and suddenly our prospective restaurant owner might be thinking, "Only 40% succeed, but I'm luckier than most people, so I think I'll be in the 40%." And if they had succeeded before, they may be tempted to think, "I'll probably be in the top of that 40%."

Here, the probabilities remain the same, but the appraisal of those probabilities varies.

As the old cliché goes, "You miss 100% of the shots you don't take." Simply believing that you are in some way luckier than average can drastically increase your likelihood of success. This is not because self-belief is a magical talisman that wins you a miracle, but because, if nothing else, it's going to motivate you to at least try. The person who doesn't try automatically *ensures* they get a poor outcome.

It's safe to say only knowing whether somebody believes in luck without knowing whether they view luck as stable or transitory does not give us enough information to properly infer how success-oriented that individual may be. But when we put the two pieces of information together, we can come to a couple of general conclusions.

An external locus of control combined with a stable view on luck will typically result in being "lucky" because they will be looking for more opportunities, similar to their counterparts with internal loci of control. They'll be *acting*.

An external locus of control combined with a fleeting view on luck will typically result in being passive, possibly also leading to a state of learned hopelessness in the absence of feeling in control. If you wanted to lose weight and you felt that nothing you did or ate would make a difference, why would you bother? In fact, if that was the rule, you might as well eat whatever you want...

Attribution Theory

Austrian psychologist Fritz Heider developed attribution theory, which deals with how we attach meaning to our own behavior and the behavior of other people – for a final look into the psychology of control and luck.

The theory states that people will attach meaning through one of two ways — internal attribution, where personality traits determine a person's success or failure; and external attribution, where a person's success or failure is the result of external circumstances. Did the salesman fail to make any sales today because he wasn't charismatic and persuasive enough, or did he simply get unlucky with difficult customers who weren't serious about making a purchase? The story you tell yourself will instantly show you where you lie on the spectrum of attribution.

It sounds similar to the loci of control theory, doesn't it?

Heider believed that we tend to view the failures of others through a lens of *internal attribution*, believing that internal personality traits caused the person's blunder. When it is instead ourselves who have erred, we are much more likely to use *external attribution* — blaming the error on situational factors or other people instead of taking personal responsibility for it.

The same theory can be applied in the case of achieving some kind of success. We will be more likely to attribute our own success internally, but the success of others externally, perhaps to "luck." When we succeed, it's because of our intelligence and charm, but when we fail, it's because of our bad luck and external circumstances. It's very convenient and defensive.

Humans are always trying to have their cake and eat it, too, being celebrated for success without being held accountable for failure. It makes sense that our attributions are determined in good part by our emotional and motivational drives. We make self-serving attributions to feel better in our success and avoid personal ramifications in our failures.

We will also tend toward self-serving attributions in the face of what we view as personal attacks. Instead of addressing the criticism, we will point to other injustices in this unfair world as distractions or excuses. This is especially true for people who have a strong need to avoid failure at all costs, as they will be most likely to make attributions that put themselves in a good light.

But are these self-serving attributions actually harming us long term? If we never take responsibility for our failures, how can we expect to learn from them and not repeat them? Furthermore, if we truly believe that luck is a major factor in our ability to succeed, then we are much less likely to have perseverance and discipline when external circumstances aren't in our favor. This is basically the logic behind making excuses and engaging in rationalizing behaviors.

We also tend to blame victims for their own suffering in a subconscious effort to distance ourselves from suffering the same plight. Yet another tendency we have is to view ourselves as more complicated than others, thinking we are more multifaceted and less predictable because we spend more of our time thinking introspectively than about the complexities of other people.

Ultimately, what can you take away from understanding these natural human tendencies?

If we prefer to think of ourselves as responsible and accountable and generally holding our own fates in our hands, then we do away completely with the concept of luck. This gives you a full path toward victory, but also failure. Perhaps we engage in lucky thinking as a defense mechanism to protect against those inevitable failures. In a way, it can be said that personal responsibility is almost directly in conflict with feelings of luck.

Take two people who have the exact same amount of talent and work equally hard. One goes out for lunch at the very moment the other is discovered by a talent agent eating lunch at his desk. Would this be considered lucky the person was simply hungry for something specific at the right moment? Would this be considered unlucky for the person who stepped out for lunch at the exact wrong moment?

Perhaps.

It might feel like this chapter has been leading up to the point of declaring that a belief in luck is going to hold you back, but that's not quite the point. It's the belief that you can't help your circumstances, and that luck will either make or break you that will hold you back. Realizing that you have the power to change your reality is what will lead to situations we would call lucky.

To whatever degree you believe in it, luck will not be the primary factor that determines the outcomes in your life. But it does matter.

Takeaways:

- Humans have an innate need to live in a world that makes sense to them, and which they feel they can control and influence. We want to predict, model and manage the world, but this combined with

our tendency to find patterns where there are none, can make our *perceptions* of probability very different from the reality.
- The way we experience and explain random events, and the cause to which we attribute these events, is highly personal. We may have an internal or external locus of control, which is whether we believe we are the cause of life's events (the former) or whether our lives are at the mercy of external events beyond our control (the latter).
- Research has discovered that there are further distinctions, and that an external locus of control can see luck as either a stable quality a person possesses, or a fleeting phenomenon that could disappear as quickly as it comes. The finding is that viewing luck as stable makes people more proactive – and more successful.
- Attribution theory deals with how we attach meaning to our own behavior and the behavior of other people. How we assign blame and praise depends on how we understand accountability and our influence on events – and it has a powerful influence on how likely we are to act and actually achieve success.

Chapter 2. What to Believe

Whatever you think of it, luck is an extremely valuable commodity because of how people seem to clamor for it. And as is the case with any valuable commodity, there are a whole lot of people who want more of it.

We've seen that when it comes to luck, there is no way to make random chance occur more frequently for us. There is (sadly!) no charm or magical incantation. But, when it comes to what we *can* change to improve our outcomes, it turns out that our attitudes, our perceptions and our beliefs make a huge difference, because they impact our behavior.

We shouldn't be at all surprised, therefore, that there are all kinds of methods out there that supposedly increase people's luck, or otherwise claim to manifest happiness and fulfillment indirectly. Whenever there is a need in a market, solutions will spring up... and not all of them are actually targeted at solving the problem. Some of them are just targeted at selling a solution.

This chapter will examine two of the most common methods of courting luck and attempt to determine if they are actually effective at bringing good fortune, or if they are merely giving people the illusion of having more control over their lives and happiness. As we've seen, luck and our perception of luck are two different things. In this book, we're attempting to genuinely move the needle, rather than go through the motions of ritual simply because they make us *feel* better.

As the chapter title notes, these are methods that may have been seen on outlets such as Oprah, or other shows that tend to hop onto new trends without regard for any scientific support. In other words, they're buzzwords and cozy ideas that might seem appealing on the surface... that is, until you dig into the science.

There may indeed be truly effective ways to be luckier in life, but are these popular notions them? Let's dive in.

The Law of Attraction

You've almost certainly encountered this principle before, whether you know it or not. The Law of Attraction is the belief that your thoughts by themselves can shape the world around you; that we can color our thoughts with emotion and feeling and those thoughts will then "manifest" themselves in our lives. The idea is that if you hold a certain end point in your mind and visualize it vividly, you magnetically draw that very thing towards you.

You might think about having a life filled with loving relationships and profound happiness, and over time, you will supposedly manifest love and happiness in your life simply because you desire it and think about it. Importantly, concrete actions are not really part of the process. The universe is thought to run on a "law" beyond conventional cause and effect, and that by adopting the energy, vibration or frequency of a particular goal, one naturally aligns with it. There are many approaches and definitions to this approach.

A Google search of the Law of Attraction will yield all kinds of results claiming that it can make a real difference in your life. The *We Shape Life Organization* breaks the method down into seven simple steps:

1. Relax your mind through 5 to 10 minutes of meditation.
2. Think about exactly what you want, creating a clear and detailed image in your mind. Don't allow yourself to have any self-doubt.
3. Ask the universe for what you want.
4. Write your wishes down and feel them happening to you.
5. Feel that your wishes are coming true. Think, speak, and act as if they already have.
6. Show gratitude by recording all of the blessings the universe has bestowed upon you.
7. Be patient and trust the universe.

You can characterize this process however you want. But then again, visualization and positive affirmations don't sound particularly promising to the skeptical mind, either, and we've already learned that there is some merit to that method. The real question is, is there any hard evidence to also support the

Law of Attraction as a legitimate method for improving one's life? Or is it pseudoscience that masquerades as self-help?

In 1999, Lien Pham and Shelley Taylor of the University of California carried out a study to test the efficacy claims of the Law of Attraction. They didn't test the exact tenets of the Law of Attraction, but essentially tested *fantastical thinking*. Fantastical thinking can be thought of as thinking about positive daydreams and fantasies and expecting that this directly impacts the external world. As you can imagine, it's no more sound than believing that a pair of stinky socks has a connection to whether you win at the casino.

But in the interests of testing the idea empirically, the researchers broke up the study's participants into three groups:

- Group 1 - Students were asked to spend a few minutes each day visualizing with a clear image how great it would feel to score highly on an important mid-term exam that was coming up in a few days.
- Group 2 - Students were asked to spend a few minutes each day visualizing when, where, and how they intended to study for the exam.

- Group 3 - This was the control group. Students were not asked to visualize anything to do with the exam.

The results were telling. The students from Group 1 studied the least and got the lowest grades on the exam. On the bright side, they did *feel better* about themselves during the process, but that is a small silver lining considering that their tangible results were contrary to what they had thought about. The results might also offer insight into the many people claiming that the law of attraction has worked for them.

Students in Group 2 who visualized themselves studying actually prepared better, studied more, and earned higher marks on the exam than the students from the other groups. They also reported that they were less stressed about the exam.

Pham and Taylor's study is another point of evidence supporting the benefits of visualization while refuting that the Law of Attraction has an ability to bring us benefit or good fortune. A simple belief in change attracting good luck may not do much good by itself, but visualizing exactly what that change entails does help.

However, one study is certainly insufficient to rule out the Law of Attraction.

A 2015 study published in the *European Journal of Social Psychology* attempted to measure the effects of implementing the Law of Attraction for students to enter romantic relationships with their crushes. A team of four researchers (Oettingen, Kappes, Guttenberg, and Gollwitzer) asked the participants to imagine what would happen in various scenarios where they interacted with their romantic crush in some way.

The researchers rated their fantasies on a spectrum from highly negative to highly positive, with some of the positive fantasies including such clichés as making eye contact across the room and knowing that it was love at first sight. The fantasies that were rated more negatively included some particularly devastating thoughts, with one girl describing her daydreaming thought as, "We are both free and single, he turns to me, smiles and asks how I am. For reasons that I still do not fully understand, I explain that I already have a boyfriend."

Five months later, the researchers reconnected with the study participants to see what had happened with their crushes in that time. On average, those students who had fantasized positively about their crushes had been *less likely* to be forthcoming about their feelings to the crush, or to otherwise pursue a relationship with them in some way, relative to those who had imagined things working out poorly.

Why? Much like the positive thinkers from the first study, these people may have felt better about themselves by fantasizing, daydreaming, and utilizing the Law of Attraction, but their positive thinking failed to manifest itself tangibly in their actual lives. Wishing for luck brought nothing but complacency. Could it be that fantasizing provided a kind of soothing temporary pseudo-outcome that made people believe that taking positive action was less urgent?

One of the researchers from the last study, Gabriele Oettingen, conducted another study measuring how positive thinking about career advancement correlated with actual career advancement over two years.

Senior college students were asked to note how often they fantasized about getting their dream job after graduation. When Oettingen followed up with the participants three years later, she learned that the students who had fantasized more frequently about career success had submitted fewer job applications, received fewer job offers, and were working for smaller salaries. It's as though the fantasies were not a stimulus for positive change but rather a replacement for it.

Based on the combined results of these three studies, it seems that the Law of Attraction may, in reality, be *detrimental*, not helpful, in manifesting what we desire to achieve in our actual lives.

Let's unpack why. Thinking positively makes us feel better, but perhaps feeling better leads to passivity. It's like using a Band-Aid and reducing the pain of a symptom while ignoring the cause of the pain itself. In other words, feeling as if we already have what we desire or that we can attain it through good luck will make us less motivated and less proactive about pursuing our goals and desires. The Law of Attraction is about belief and thought, and even visualization emphasizes process and detail. Proponents of the law of attraction are sometimes explicitly told to relax and assume that the problem is already being solved behind the scenes. This reduces tension and urgency, which may feel better in the short term. What it doesn't do, however, is move anyone forward.

So what can we do to take advantage of positive thinking and the power of our minds? And how can we do this without succumbing to pleasant fantasy and wishful thinking?

Wishing or fantasizing that we reach our goals and attain all of our desires without action doesn't seem to do anything but harm us. But visualizing taking the actions to make those things happen actually makes us more likely to be proactive. So, the quality and content of our fantasies matter. While our positive ideas, thoughts, and dreams can help us determine what we want, by themselves, they don't necessarily lead to action or good luck.

The Law of Attraction is still being pushed because people want to believe that they can achieve everything they desire without putting in the time and effort to actually make it happen, but unfortunately, that remains an unrealistic and impossible dream. In fact, entertaining and indulging the lazy human desire for reward without effort may make it even more likely that you'll end up with an outcome you don't want.

The bottom line is, creating "good luck" in our lives is really more about creating the conditions for positive things to happen to us. If you want to work at your dream job and make a higher salary, you'll need to put in the effort to apply for jobs, work hard, and build up your skills and networking connections to realistically qualify yourself for that dream job.

How do you apply the method of visualization and affirmation to reaching goals that are more abstract than shooting free throws better, or not getting stressed out about taking a test? Easy: embrace the process or journey of reaching your goals, rather than focusing on the destination. A few examples will clarify.

Let's say you really want to get into better shape so that you can show off your swimsuit body on your next tropical vacation. Imagining yourself with the body you want won't help you get it, but visualizing yourself working out in the gym or hiking a nearby mountain path just might increase the chances that you actually do those things. Repeating self-affirmations that you are disciplined and hard-working and that you will stick to your exercise regimen — even on the days you feel tired or discouraged — can build your belief in yourself to accomplish your goals. Again, you are creating the conditions for luck, not the positive outcome itself. You are imagining the intermediate steps that carry you to a goal, rather than focusing on the goal itself with no thought for the practical way that the goal comes about.

Fantasy and daydreaming *can* be useful. But daydreams mean nothing if they're not tethered to reality somehow. A fantastically imagined visualization might yield valuable insights or help you better understand what you want. But when you're done daydreaming, you'll still need to grapple with material reality to make the changes necessary.

If you want to give yourself a mental boost, visualize yourself working through the process of reaching that destination or reward. The real magic is in building up the internal belief that you are capable of creating the conditions for "luck," not that your beliefs can manifest luck into your life in and of themselves. This is really an extreme external locus of control dressed up as an internal locus of control. Good luck doesn't come around just by wishing and waiting for it, as much as we may want it to.

The Self-Fulfilling Prophecy

Robert K. Merton, a 20th-century sociologist, may have coined this term, but examples of this can be found in literature as far back as ancient Greece and ancient India. The concept is one that is familiar to most people, as they've likely witnessed it unfolding in their own lives. The self-fulfilling prophecy is basically a prediction that directly or indirectly *causes itself* to become true due to positive feedback between belief and behavior.

Put simply, this is the idea that a positive or negative prophecy, strongly held belief, or delusion can sufficiently influence people so that their reactions ultimately fulfill the prophecy itself. The classic story of Oedipus, for example, wherein a father had a prophecy that his son was going to kill him, sent him away to prevent it, but the sending away resulted in the very series of actions that led to his death. A more everyday example is a person who is so worried about making a bad first impression at an interview that they stay up all night stressing about it, oversleep, and then make a bad impression at the interview the next morning because they're tired and anxious.

This leads to the *behavioral confirmation event*, in which behaviors that are influenced by expectations cause those very expectations to come true. You may go to an interview, completely blow it, and come home thinking, "see? I knew it."

If you think about it, this isn't a hard idea to grasp. If someone expects something of you, whether it be good or bad, you will live up to that expectation more often than not. We are no longer in the murky realms of luck and probability, but simply playing, again, with *perception and expectation* – which turn out to play a massive role in what we think of as luck. If you believe you have bad luck, you will act in a way that will ensure bad luck will enter your life, and so on. You create the cycle in which you live through the power of your thoughts and intentions.

I can still remember my very first work presentation that I had to deliver to a group of colleagues about some research I had done. Logically, I knew that my work was fine and that all my data was correct. However, this wasn't as easy to convince myself of in practice. I was so certain that I would forget a point or speak too quietly and make a complete fool of myself. On the day, I found myself trying to do the complete opposite. This resulted in a speech that was mostly yelled, far too long, and excruciatingly slow. I looked and sounded insane. This is a perfect example of how a belief, particularly a negative one, can focus someone's attention and cause the very thing they feared to begin with.

In the case of luck, if you believe you have bad luck, you will ignore every positive thing that occurs and focus blindly on everything that is negative. This is something we all do. You may have had a perfectly ordinary day at work, but as soon as you make one error, it suddenly feels like your whole day starts to turn into a disaster. Often, this is because focusing on the negatives will cause you to act in a way that is contrary to what generates good luck. Instead of being open-minded and willing to explore new possibilities, you let tunnel vision take over, and your fear shuts you down.

A self-fulfilling prophesy can be so powerful that it even causes us to interpret positive outcomes as negative ones, if it means they align with our catastrophic predictions. For example, you may be so convinced of your bad luck in love that you come away from a neutral or even positive first date and then deliberately decide it was a flop, and never contact the person again. They disappear from your life, and you will never know if they might have been the love of your life had you waited to go on a second date. You tell others, "I'm unlucky in love." And because you believe so, it's true. The funny thing is how closely this resembles the law of attraction, while essentially being the very opposite!

Bad luck isn't always centered on an event or situation. Plenty of people are certain that they have a particular object that is the sole reason behind every "bad luck" incident in their lives. Perhaps it's a pair of socks (or absence thereof) that you just know is behind all your troubles, or a song that is always playing when you have a particularly embarrassing moment. Some people are convinced they are forever jinxed by their unattractive name, a weird physical feature, or some random fact of their past.

Whatever it is, if you believe something will give or bring you bad luck, you will undoubtedly begin to act differently around it, fixate on it in an unhealthy way, and ultimately act differently than you normally would. You may feel that your acne is single-handedly ruining your social life, and so you avoid eye contact, and squirm uncomfortably when people look at you – which is a great way to ruin your social life! It is because you act differently and out of your normal flow or behavior that things may seem to just fall apart, just like an athlete who overthinks his game strategy and ends up ruining it all.

If you believe you have great luck, you are more likely to create it — not out of thin air, and not by magic, but by not driving away beneficial situations. The lucky rabbit's foot you carry in your pocket has no magical powers, but if it causes you to smile, think positively and have faith that you can come up with proactive and creative solutions, then it *is*, in effect, a lucky rabbit's foot.

The power of belief

Tennessee Williams once said, "luck is believing you are lucky."

It's a heavy irony. Wishful thinking doesn't create good outcomes, but believing it does will. So, it's worth believing in luck, despite its not existing! Rather than a supernatural force or a random event, luck is best thought of as a *subjective interpretation* of neutral events that has a concrete influence over how those events play out.

A belief in luck can lead to a "virtuous cycle" – i.e., a loop of confirmation that ends up creating the narrative it believes exists. Counterintuitively, believing you are lucky makes you work harder and make better plans. Even better, believing you are lucky makes you pay more attention to emerging opportunities and possible solutions so that you're better able to capitalize than those who believe they have rotten luck.

Richard Wiseman at the University of Herefordshire is the author of the 2003 book *The Luck Factor*. He conducted an experiment where he asked participants to count pictures in a newspaper. At the same time, he "hid" the solution to the puzzle on the second page of that newspaper. He noticed that the participants who considered themselves lucky people were more likely to notice the solution than those who considered themselves cursed with bad luck.

So, in a weird plot twist, the people who thought they were lucky... were!

You may start to notice these effects in people around you. Someone may plan ahead and pack tissues in their bag and, when someone gets a nosebleed, triumphantly presents the tissues and says, "look at that! How lucky." You may notice that the pessimistic people who always grumble and say, "huh, just my luck!" are also the ones who seem to do very little to improve their situation, or actively blame the outcomes of their failure to act on some supernatural force that has a mysterious grudge on them. Such people may even unconsciously jeopardize themselves and invite failure just so they can confirm their belief in themselves as unfortunate.

Economist Alan Kirman of the École des Hautes Études en Sciences Sociales in Paris has conducted a few studies into the random things we consider lucky breaks, like finding a parking spot. He discovered that people might be trapped in bad luck spirals without consciously knowing what's happening. Our perceptions and attributions can compound and reinforce themselves via our behavior, so that we eventually start to feel like the world really is against us – even though we are the ones bringing about those outcomes. People might, for instance, believe that certain people are just lucky when it comes to spotting great parking spaces, but believe this to such an extent that they actually "learn to choose the spots far back and leave the spots for other spots for the guys who are 'lucky.'" Perception really matters!

In addition to using visualization to imagine yourself taking concrete steps towards your goal, try to incorporate affirmations to cement a belief in yourself as a lucky person. Don't overthink it. Even if you don't actually believe it, tell yourself that pretending to believe will still have the desired effect. Regularly tell yourself things like:

"I'm a lucky person."

"This obstacle is obviously only a temporary glitch."

"I'm pretty resourceful and good at spotting opportunities."

"There's always a silver lining."

"Good things tend to happen to me."

The people who consider themselves lucky? Kirman discovered that they seemed to share a constellation of attitudes and perspectives that included a general optimism, a determination not to dwell on mistakes from the past, and a willingness to listen to their gut intuition. Richard Wiseman has even created a "Luck School" where he trains people to cultivate these precise attitudes. Remarkably, 80% of the "unlucky" people who attended this school claimed afterwards that they were happier and luckier.

Finally, there is a habit that self-described lucky people tend to indulge in, and that's a particular interpretation of even negative events. For example, if a car races by you in the road and narrowly avoids running you down, you could say, "I'm so unlucky, I almost died!" or you could say, "How lucky am I? I could have died but didn't!" This is so-called counterfactual thinking, and it's associated with being more grateful, being happier and feeling that you're luckier in general. It's the willingness to put a light rosy tint on your interpretation of events, which doesn't exactly change those events, but may well influence subsequent events. For example, if you think you are lucky to have escaped death, you may feel so much more grateful for your life, and the "second chance" you've been given, that you go out of your way to take care of yourself and avoid risks. You thereby prolong your life and may actually live longer, especially when compared to a person who unconsciously felt that death was always lurking around the corner.

Imagining an alternative life path in which you didn't experience a lucky outcome you currently enjoy summons up powerful feelings of gratitude and optimism. And it comes from simply reframing events to focus on what is actually quote fortunate already.

At the start of this chapter, we investigated whether something like the law of attraction actually has any evidence to back it up. We found none. However, if the law of attraction inadvertently made you believe that you were a luckier person than most, and this then caused you to subtly but powerfully shift your behavior in the world. One could then argue that *belief* in the theory had some positive outcomes, even if the theory itself is worthless. Lady Luck turns out to be a tricky customer after all!

Takeaways:

- There are two popular ideas worth exploring when it comes to the concept of luck: the law of attraction, and the idea of a self-fulfilling prophesy. Research into the effectiveness of the law of attraction (or wishful thinking) yields no support,

and indicates that fantasy can actually undermine success by making us less likely to take useful action.
- A self-fulfilling prophecy is a prediction that directly or indirectly *causes itself* to become true due to positive feedback between belief and behavior. It proves how powerful belief can be.
- If you believe you are a lucky person, you are more likely to create that reality yourself — not out of thin air, or by magic, but because you are proactively taking steps to make that outcome a reality.
- Robert Wiseman and Alan Kirman have independently discovered that being lucky may come down to believing that you are lucky.
- Lucky people do visualize, yet they tend to imagine not the outcome but the performance of the practical steps needed to reach that outcome. They tend to be positive and optimistic, easily forget past mistakes, trust their gut feelings, and put a positive interpretation on events by imagining how things could have been so much worse. This, in effect, means that people who believe they're lucky, are!

Chapter 3. What to Think

It might seem like lucky is something you are born to be. Fortunately, being lucky is not just about the accidents of your birth, innate ability, or even talent. If there's been a theme throughout this book thus far, it is that luckiness is achievable through *creating conditions for luck* — and that is wholly within your control.

Truly being lucky boils down to a short aphorism by the Roman philosopher and statesman, Seneca: "Luck is where opportunity meets preparation."

In Ancient Rome, Seneca lived a life that defined luck. He was born into a low rank, but through his hard work and awareness, he moved up into the realm of the elite in Rome. His "luck" brought him a friendship with Roman emperors, including Claudius and

Nero. He eventually became one of the wealthiest people of his day.

Was Seneca luckier than most people? He certainly wasn't unlucky. But he also understood the workings of the world, which is clear throughout the philosophical texts he crafted in his lifetime. He embodied several of the traits that modern researchers and psychologists consider to be those of lucky people.

Some people may find that money falls in their lap or a lucky break comes from nowhere, and they find their fortunes turning with no input from them. But this kind of luck ("dumb" luck?) is by definition pretty uncommon, and since we can't create t for ourselves, it's not worth thinking about. But as we've seen, there are other, subtler grey areas between "100% dumb luck" and "hard work." In that realm where our attitude, preparation, actions, and perceptions change how we maximize the random opportunities we're given, we have more control than we think. We've seen that lucky people are optimistic and believe they're lucky. Let's look at a few more traits that the lucky have in common.

Lucky Traits

There are a handful of traits that are common in people who consider themselves to be lucky.

Richard Wiseman, the psychologist we encountered earlier, has extensively studied luck, and found that people who are lucky find themselves in a certain state of mind that makes them more aware of lucky occurrences. You can call it a lucky mindset, or simply the tendency to get themselves into situations many people would call lucky. Luck, then, is a complex mix of attribution, perception and deliberate positive action. In several experiments relating to luck, he found that those who achieve it tend to have three consistent personality traits.

Those three personality traits for luck include variations on the spectrums of extroversion, openness, and neuroticism. Wiseman found that people with those three traits weren't exactly more blessed or fortunate (that would be quite the scientific finding!) but rather that their outlook made them *available to opportunities* that turned into lucky moments. The same opportunities that, ostensibly, we're all exposed to in equal measure. These three traits seemed to give people a better chance at being in the right place at the right time and maximizing their opportunities for great outcomes.

Extroversion

Extroversion is the first trait Wiseman found to be highly correlated with luck.

According to the *Big 5 Factors theory* of personality, extroversion is defined by people being assertive, energetic, and talkative. Extroversion is associated with comfort with social interaction and a tendency to move towards other people and new situations. Someone who shows extroversion is likely to be lucky due to an enthusiastic involvement with the outside world. It's easy to imagine why: extroverts have an easy time talking to anyone, so they often have opportunities to meet interesting people. How many times have you heard people describe a lucky encounter that essentially came down to them chatting up the right person by accident? These are opportunities that more shy or withdrawn people might never take advantage of.

Extroverts become highly energized when they are around other people. They are likely to become the life of any party. They are easy to notice in crowds because of their talkative and energetic personalities, which could explain why lucky things happen to them. If we take luck to be a quantity that increases with exposure and experience, extroverts are necessarily luckier because they crave that exposure, and tend to put themselves more frequently into varied situations. The more opportunities you come across, even bad ones, the more you increase your exposure to a lucky chance encounter. The more you try, the more you discover and experience. Simply, you're going to have more lucky breaks when you meet ten people a day versus none.

Let's be honest: luck very often comes from other people doing something for or with us. Our social connections can create our lucky breaks, our pivotal moments, and occasionally save our hides! It stands to reason then that those with more social connections will have more channels through which this kind of luck can flow to them.

If you find yourself the aloof or retiring type, you may discover more luck comes your way when you open up to other people. Tell others what you're struggling with and what you need – you never know when or from where help may be spontaneously offered. Speak enthusiastically about your passions so that other people will help you connect to others who can help or join you on your mission. Most importantly, pay attention and be a good listener – luck often arrives simply because you knew a valuable piece of information you might have otherwise missed.

Open-Mindedness

When someone demonstrates a high level of openness, they are relaxed about life and ready to experience new circumstances. They are receptive and open to following emerging threads, rather than shutting themselves off to new possibilities or solutions. They are not as risk-averse as others and don't make decisions through a perspective of fear and anxiety. When opportunity knocks on the door of someone with an open mind, that person will answer the door and investigate the challenge. They'll not only open the door, but they'll walk down that path and consider if they even want to return the way they came. Someone with a closed mind will not do any of these things. Simply give yourself more opportunities for luck to occur.

It is relatively easy to identify someone who has a high level of openness; this is the person who doesn't say no to anything, whether you suggest it or they do. Let's say you want to go skydiving, but you want to go with a friend. The friend who is open to new ideas is the one you will call.

Open people tend to land in the luckiest circumstances. They end up with the best jobs because they make themselves aware of opportunities. They'll be the person who always seems to have a funny story of coincidence or chance encounters that lead to amazing adventures. They also seem to be the people who end up backstage at concerts, with the autographs at ballparks, and as winners in contests. These things happen to them because they are open to opportunities, and they jump on them. They may not readily identify everything as a positive opportunity, but just as importantly, they don't rule anything out.

If this attitude is not your strong suit, you may find yourself feeling luckier if you can simply relax and include more spontaneity in your life. Shift your perspective from *why* to *why not?* Accept invitations, try something unexpected and be willing to see the upside in an outcome you didn't quite plan for.

Low Neuroticism

Finally, neuroticism is technically a state of being *neurotic*, which often includes anxiety, nervousness, and jealousy. Essentially, this is the trait of being high-strung and perpetually on guard. Unlike the other two traits, Wiseman found that those at the opposite end, with low-levels of neuroticism, were likely to have more luck in their lives than those at the high-level end.

Why is this?

Someone who shows low levels of neuroticism will be calmer and more relaxed than someone at the high end of the spectrum. When people are calm and focused, they become highly aware of their surroundings without being anxious. They do not scan the environment looking for threats, and tend to interpret neutral situations favorably, rather than find them intimidating. Someone in a relaxed state of mind allows themselves to be open to opportunity and even happiness, whereas someone who is perpetually anxious will be endlessly preoccupied with perceived slights, insults, and alarms. It comes down to a sense of expectation – a neurotic person expects bad things to happen, while a relaxed and non-neurotic one is calm, comfortable and broadly faces life with curiosity.

Someone with low neuroticism also sees what is happening around them, and is therefore often lucky. For example, while many people walk down the street listening to music or focusing on their phones, the low neuroticism person will often walk down the street, taking in the ambiance and the view. They don't feel threatened by letting their guards down. This is why people with low neuroticism become so lucky — because they are paying attention to the world and choosing not to become closed off to it. When their minds are not preoccupied with anxiety, they are able to be present and explore what's in front of them.

One of Wiseman's studies clearly showed how openness and awareness can play a major factor in what we consider "luck." Remember the newspaper experiment? Wiseman asked volunteers to count the number of photographs in a newspaper. On page two of the newspaper, there was a headline that read

"STOP COUNTING—THERE ARE 43 PHOTOGRAPHS IN THIS NEWSPAPER." Further down the page was another headline that read, "STOP COUNTING, TELL THE EXPERIMENTER YOU HAVE SEEN THIS AND WIN $250."

Everyone in the study missed the headlines, but they did count all 43 photographs. Wiseman concluded that people were too focused (too neurotic) on the goal. They failed to relax and see the opportunities that were right in front of their faces. This goes to show that sometimes, our preconceived notions about how things should play out, and our need to control and fixate on tasks and a particular interpretation shut us out to the magical possibility of something *better* happening. Often, being lucky is simply a question of getting gout of your own way, and allowing that luck to find you!

Even though these three personality traits contribute to lucky events, the real reason people tend to be lucky is that they are involved in the world around them. Like Seneca said, it takes work. But Wiseman found that along with work, relaxation helps too. People who try too hard to find opportunities miss them more often than not because they end up making themselves blind to anything else. So, when it comes luck, a balance between being relaxed and alert helps. This is the balance between being open, calm, and extroverted.

Recall that luck is mostly random and is only somewhat self-generated. No one can predict what will happen to them, but a person can manage their reactions to those events. Being calm and relaxed, open to opportunities, and involved in life makes it easier to jump on those random events and become "lucky." We cannot create good fortune, but we can invite it in.

In addition to these traits, optimism is a driver of good fortune. Optimists look at the bright side of life, seeking the bright side and anticipating that good things will happen. Lucky people tend to be optimists because they act like they are going to succeed. For instance, you will prepare for a long car ride far differently than you would prepare for a 10-minute ride. The way you view something drastically changes your actions.

Along with adding optimism to your daily routine, it is helpful to develop a sense of humility. If you are not afraid of being embarrassed in unexpected situations, then you will be open and free to try new things. By being calm and accepting that you might fail, you will be surprised by the good things that come your way. If you are instead defensiveness and afraid of judgment and rejection, you will probably close yourself off from most chances for luck because the cost (embarrassment) simply won't be worth the benefit (an opportunity). A little bit of vulnerability can make you far luckier if you are just willing to take a leap of faith more frequently.

Take, for example, the professional baseball player. Every time a professional baseball player goes up to bat, he has a roughly 72% chance of failing in front of hundreds of thousands of people on TV and in the stadium. But he expects it and is okay with the potential for failure. If the baseball player did not take that chance of failure, he could never become the hero who hits the big home run to win the game. At the plate, the batter has to be calm, optimistic, vulnerable, and completely ready to accept failure. This also underlies openness.

Optimism means you resist labelling outcomes as failures simply because they weren't what you wanted, and instead see how every change in your circumstances could be welcomed as a positive opportunity for something new. Sometimes, we are so focused on what has gone wrong that we don't see a great chance sitting right in front of us!

Finally, you can change your luck by being proactive. Being lucky involves more than just showing up; you actually have to get engaged in life. You have to search for opportunities, because they will not land in your lap if you are not out there seeking them (well, they *might*, but waiting for them alone is not going to make them happen any faster than they were going to!).

Along with Seneca and Machiavelli's words of wisdom, the Latin aphorism "Carpe Diem" is another excellent way to live a lucky life. This aphorism is a proclamation to live life to the fullest, grasping the present moment in front of you while you can. Instead of shying away for fear of looking silly or the possibility of failing, lucky people try new things and give it their best shot. They act where others are hesitant, or unprepared, fearful, or still ruminating over the past.

When you get involved with life, sometimes you win, and sometimes you lose. But do you skip taking a vacation because you are afraid of the small chance the plane could crash with you on it? If you don't get on the plane, then you do not get to see the world. If you do not buy the lottery card, then you cannot win the $1 million prize. If we let fear keep us back, then we miss out on all of the wonderful things that could happen. The old "shoulda-coulda-woulda" syndrome.

Luck doesn't come to those people who said, "I wish I would have taken that job," or "I should have gone on that date," or "If only I could have another chance, I would do it differently." How could it? No lucky break is so powerful that it will barge into your life even though you're doing your best to shut it out.

No, luck comes to people who take the job, go on the date, and do it the first time. Luck presents itself in random ways, and it is up to you to recognize it and accept the opportunity. The universe speaks in mysterious ways, and we cannot open our eyes to it if we are always worried about the plane crashing.

Richard Wiseman saw the power of mindset in the very different people in his research. In his psychological studies to understand why some people are luckier than others, he has presented strangers with opportunities that many would consider lucky. He has literally placed luck right in front of them in many situations. Some completely miss it. But others immediately spot the opportunity. It has nothing to do with "luck" but everything to do with being receptive to opportunity.

Lucky thought patterns
Being extroverted, open-minded, relaxed and positive will mean you are luckier. But lucky people don't just possess certain traits, they also demonstrate specific patterns of thinking and ways of looking at the world. Remember, though, that this is not quite the same as practicing the law of attraction or indulging in wishful thinking. Rather, your attitudes and beliefs are what cause particular kinds of behaviors in you, and it's these behaviors that lead to an optimal relationship with randomness and chance in the world around you.

The first thought pattern that we'll consider may seem counterintuitive: karma.

Luck and karma

In Buddhist and Hindu thought, karma is a belief that people's "fortunes" are, in sum, a total of their previous actions and deeds, typically actions that occurred in a previous incarnation. Karma is the law of cause and effect, and the word literally means action or deed. While the Western interpretation of this concept tends towards the moralistic, and sees outcomes as either rewards or punishments, the karmic conception sees results as neither good nor bad. Instead, the law is seen neutrally, a little like the law of gravity. If we act in certain ways, we set external events in motion. Who we are today rests entirely on the decisions and actions we have made in the past.

You might be wondering – doesn't this idea directly contradict the idea of random chance and luck?

Well, yes. But recall that we are examining certain outlooks and mental mindsets that are *functional*, not considering their truth or accuracy. Just as we saw that believing you are lucky tends to make you so (without magically changing the material facts of the universe), believing in karma may be a way to prime yourself mentally for a more serendipitous life.

How? Recall that people who have an extrinsic locus of control, and especially those that see luck as fleeting, will adopt a passive, apathetic and resigned orientation to life. They will not take action because, well, there's no point. Effort is not rewarded, and benefits are bestowed randomly. However, this mindset leads to us forfeiting our ability to act and change our worlds.

If you believe in karma, though, you will take action very seriously. If, to you, the universe seems ordered on consistent and logical principles of cause and effect, you will take care of the causes you are creating, lest you get an unwanted effect. In other words, you will behave in the best possible way to bring about good things in your life.

If someone believes, "If I do good deeds, more good luck will come my way," then how will they act? They'll likely do good deeds. They may help those in need, speak with kindness, and forgive wrongs. They'll try to bravely endure adversity and do their best in every situation. They'll try to redeem negative patterns from the past, learn from mistakes and overcome their limitations. You can see where this is going!

Around 2004 there were disastrous tidal waves in the Indian Ocean, and thousands upon thousands of people were killed. A holy teacher was asked if those who died did so because of their karma. The teacher said, "they were in the wrong place at the wrong time. But how well they fared against those tidal waves *was* down to their karma." In other words, the mental imprints and mindsets those people had determined their *response* to a chaotic and random event.

While luck and karma seem like opposites, the Buddhists do recognize the power of chance events – but they also know that we always have agency, and that our conditioning, our imprints from the past, and the momentum from the actions we've taken also play a massive role.

When you act from a belief that everything you do either takes you closer to or further from an enlightened state, you adopt an internal locus of control and behave with extreme optimism. You choose those behaviors that are most likely to win you the cooperation, respect and help of those around you – i.e., being kind, compassionate and generous. More than that, you will take responsibility for your action, and not grow apathetic or lose hope.

One day you forgive a colleague for an insult, telling yourself that everyone gets what they deserve in the end. Two years later, that colleague is in another job and now in the perfect position to help you in your career – and they remember your kindness and want to pay it back. Now, was it the law of karma that got this lucky result, or was it the *belief* in the law of karma, and your subsequent choice to act with forgiveness?

Luck and resilience

If you keep showing up and don't get discouraged, you will encounter more opportunities, and it's more likely that one of those opportunities will develop into success. Someone may go to 10 auditions and get nowhere, and decide to quit completely. Another person may also go to 10 auditions, and find their lucky break on the 11th. They are not luckier than the first person; they just held out for longer.

The saying goes that the master has failed more times than the beginner has even tried. The only difference between them is determination. While someone might envy the person who was lucky enough to have their book snatched up by a publisher, they may not notice that that person has been sending their manuscripts to publishers *for years*, and getting mountains of rejection letters. They carried on submitting manuscripts long after most people gave up because they had "no luck."

To stay dedicated in the face of adversity of challenge requires resilience. And while this seems on the surface like a character trait, it's more of a belief that goes something like, "I can handle this. Better things are coming." Like the belief in karma, believing that our actions will eventually be rewarded is also a key part of staying dedicated.

It comes down to action. We cannot control random chance events, but what we can control, we can do so via our concrete actions in the real world. It follows then that the person who can sustain useful action for as long as possible will see more luck come their way than the person who acts a little, but gives up. Many successful people will bristle slightly at the suggestion that they've been lucky, because they know that the person saying so has not seen the sleepless nights, the hard work, the failures, and the persistence behind the "luck."

Resilience does *not* mean that someone is better able to cope with adversity, or has more stamina. It does not mean that they have some secret ability that others don't. All it means is that they have an optimal way of *perceiving* failure and challenge. People who are resilient get their energy from the fact that they have faith in their own abilities. Dr Ginsburg is an expert on child development and the subject of resilience in the face of trauma, and he finds that there are 7 parts to having grit and being strong in the face of trouble:

Competence ("I know how to do this")

Confidence ("I can do this")

Connection ("I'm not doing this alone")

Character ("I'm a good person with high self-esteem")

Contribution ("I have a part to play in the world")

Coping ("I can survive stress")

Control ("I am in charge of my actions and decisions")

In fact, if you read the above statements out loud, it's hard not to stand a little taller and feel like you'll be OK, no matter what!

Luck and learning

Finally, while we're on the topic of taking action and taking charge, let's mention the role of learning in creating more luck in your life. We've seen that an external locus of control and a resigned attitude will always fail to make the best of opportunities. Again and again, it seems that the path to a luckier life is in what you *do*, and the decisions you make.

But of course, indiscriminate or even useless action won't get you anyway. Action, if it's to bring us into more contact with beneficial chance encounters, needs to make sense. Lucky people don't just act and then close their eyes and wish for the best. They act, notice the effect their actions have had, and adjust accordingly.

Always be aware of your circumstances and how they are changing with the choices you make. Look carefully at what is actually bringing you luck, and what is just a useless gesture, like crossing your fingers and hoping passively for a miracle. See what works, then do whatever you can to create those same conditions again. In other words, be intelligent about the way you coax and invite fortuitous events into your world.

Lucky people engage with the results of their actions and notice what works. And, because they have faith in their abilities and believe that their actions matter, they are ready and willing to adjust, adapt, evolve or switch things up when needed. It could be as simple as noticing that you often get a coffee on the house when you go to your favorite café in the morning, and a particular barista is behind the counter. So that's when you go, and that's how you get more free coffees in your life.

It could be realizing that every successful relationship you've ever had has been with someone you met through friends, and not online. Now, by shifting where you focus your energies when finding a mate, you apparently increase your "luck" and find someone amazing faster. In this way, learning from what works and what doesn't is a way to take a lucky break and run with it, essentially *learning* how to be luckier. If you get a heads up on a brilliant new available property that's not yet been advertised, and you nab that property before anyone else, you might realize, "wait a second. When you have good relationships with people in the know, you can get a lucky break without much effort." How much luck could you find for yourself in the world if you consistently applied this lesson, and befriended those people who would also have inside information when it counted?

In this case, the thought pattern is, "XYZ worked! Now how can I make that happen again?" This train of thought takes optimism and gratitude (to recognize when you've been lucky), awareness (to notice how and why it happened), and proactive self-belief (the faith that if you take the right actions, you'll get a similar result). What it doesn't take is a belief in dumb luck and a thought that goes, "XYZ worked! What a fluke. Well, that was nice, but I wonder when the next disaster will happen…"

Wiseman's three personality traits for luck can be more accurately said to create situations for luck to thrive. And believing in karma, having resilience, or being ready to learn and adapt also creates the mindset that invites more luck in. You can embody these traits and thought patterns yourself, in small ways – or you can deliberately cultivate a mindset that amplifies the negative and makes sure that when opportunities come, you never see or grasp them!

Seneca was on to something when he realized that recognizing opportunities is the key to finding luck. It happens when you seize the moment and don't let fear get in the way. Believe in yourself, take action, and learn to master what works. Relax, stay calm, look around, and take the chance when the chance arrives.

Summary:

- Seneca famously said, "luck is where preparation meets opportunity." There is plenty we can do to prepare ourselves so that we are ready to notice and seize new opportunities that emerge, and make ourselves more "lucky."
- There are three main traits associated with being a lucky person. The first is extroversion, which leads us to engage with others socially, speak out, make connections and win others over. This will naturally create more opportunities for help, random connections, or new information that can spell a lucky break.
- The second trait is open-mindedness, which is a receptive, spontaneous state of mind that approaches life with curiosity rather than fear, bias or expectation. With openness to new experiences, we say yes to new opportunities and encounter more life experiences that have the chance to evolve favorably.
- The third trait is low neuroticism. When we are relaxed and not acting from fear,

we see solutions, think outside the box and encounter unexpected positive outcomes – and we don't jeopardize any good luck we do encounter!
- There are three thought patterns associated with being lucky. Believing in karma means you take your actions seriously and are more likely to have a proactive internal locus of control, and treat others well – naturally leading to more luck opportunities.
- Belief in your own competence and ability to withstand adversity creates resilience, meaning you take beneficial action for longer, which means you increase your chances of a positive outcome.
- Finally, lucky people learn what works and deliberately try to recreate those conditions that they know have led to luck for them in the past.

Chapter 4. What To Do

So, we've looked closely at what to think, how to be, and what traits to cultivate in yourself so that you are maximizing on whatever brilliant opportunities the universe is throwing your way. If luck = preparation + opportunity, then we have the following two components that make up luck:

Opportunity – we cannot control this, but we can control ourselves, and adopt a positive, open-minded, relaxed and proactive mindset so that we can make the best of existing opportunity and be receptive to new opportunity.

Preparation – we can take action, i.e. *do* something, whether in response to an opportunity or in preparation for it.

The right mindset will naturally lead to the right actions, which is why we spent so much time exploring the way that lucky people's attitudes and personalities differ from unlucky people's. But as is probably clear to you by now, action matters – a lot – and so it's worth also exploring the quintessential behaviors that set lucky people apart. What exactly do they **do**, day in and day out, that puts them on a different, luckier path in life?

Task 1: Work harder
This should come as no surprise! It goes against our conventional understanding of a lucky person (i.e., someone who has nice things just fall into their laps), but the unglamorous truth is that lucky people work hard. Really hard. True, you might hear a story of some amazing opportunity coming to find someone while they were doing something else, but usually that "something else" was working hard on another goal, related or not.

Lucky people lean into the "preparation" part of the above equation, and they do everything they can to invite and keep luck in their life. Once they catch a lucy break, they milk it for everything it's worth. Not everything they do leads directly to results, but it doesn't have to, and they don't expect it to. Imagine a wildlife photographer who wins a prize for an absolutely phenomenal shot of a bird caught midflight catching an insect. The picture captures a moment of perfect timing, but conceals that the photographer took dozens (or hundreds!) or imperfect photos, and even then, the chosen pic was edited, cropped and tweaked further.

Imagine, too, that this photograph had been entered unsuccessfully into several competitions over the course of years, and that it represents countless conversations about those competitions, advice garnered from industry professionals, hours spent in photography courses, and weekend evenings devoted to learning how to use photo editing software.

Now imagine even further that one day this person is at an awards event because of this picture they took, and here they meet a person they instantly click with. This person loves the photographer's portfolio and is really impressed with the passion and enthusiasm that they have when talking about their work. Spontaneously, they say, "Hey, I'm working on this new film project, and I'd love to have someone like you on our team. What do you say?" And just like that, another related but completed unexpected opportunity opens up, and our esteemed photographer now has the chance to expand their skills into the film-making world.

It's luck, yes. But luck riding on the back of lots and lots of hard work. Meeting the film maker at the awards event was pure chance. But there were two things that made the photographer able to grasp that chance and run with it: the cumulative results of all the work they'd done so far (i.e., the winning photo) and their enthusiasm when talking about their photography passion (more on this in just a moment).

Whatever it is you're trying to achieve, put in the hours. Imagine you are laying the groundwork so that when your chance arrives, everything is in place, ready and waiting for it. Create and build things that you can point to with pride. Practice a skill that is valuable to others and can be transferred to other areas of life (like coding, public speaking, a new language or even general business skills). If you are an artist or creative like the photographer above, build your portfolio so that you have something to show promising people who wander into your life.

If you're launching a new business, fine-tune your "elevator pitch" or print business cards –

you may never use them, but *not* having them ready when/if you need them will cost you far more than it costs to do it just in case. Save up money, educate yourself, and put in the practice hours. Keep up with events in your area of passion or expertise. Keep showing up. Even if it doesn't immediately feel like it, by doing so you are making daily contributions to an investment that may well pay off one day. Remember, though, to maintain the right mindset: keep reminding yourself that your efforts do have an impact, and that you may need to be resilient and patient enough to hang in there until that impact manifests. Remember, also, that effort needs to be intelligent. Keep consistent and don't give up, but if something genuinely isn't working, don't be afraid to adapt and try something else!

Task 2: Use the luck surface area theory

Let's return to our photographer friend, and imagine that things had played out a little differently for him. Let's imagine that he worked really hard to hone his craft, took pains to take an amazing photo, submitted it everywhere and then won the award at the ceremony. And then went home. Or, imagine that he stayed, but since he felt intimidated by all the people there and a little unconfident in himself, he spent the evening being a phony, i.e., trying to impress others by talking about the things he thought he was supposed to talk about. Noticing everyone was a film maker, he launches into the discussions about various films but comes across as insecure and a faker (remember self-fulfilling prophecies?). The people at the ceremony aren't really impressed and forget about him soon after.

He put in just as much hard work as in our previous example, but in this story, he doesn't meet the film maker who offers him the opportunity of a lifetime. The dominos set in motion by his initial hard work stop falling, and the luck runs out.

What's happened here?

According to the "surface area" theory of luck, he's reduced his overall *exposure* to luck. The hard work stayed the same, but something else disappeared from the equation.

The truth is that success is not a linear path, and lucky breaks emerge when a special *combination* of forces come together to make them possible. Hard work, grit and resilience, education, knowing how to hustle, perseverance, connections... which matters most? Well, they all matter, when they work together.

Enter Jason Roberts, who coined the term "luck surface area." To put it briefly, luck surface area is the degree of action to take concerning your passion *plus* the number of people you share that passion with. In other words, action plus communication. Like for our photographer, his success resulted from a combination of his persistent hard work, and the effective communication of his passion with the people that mattered. How do you know which people will matter? Well, you don't. That's why you have to communicate your passion to as many people as possible!

His equation goes as follows: **Luck = Doing x Telling**

Basically, luck is a result of the interaction between acting towards your passion, and speaking up to others about it. Imagine a graph where the x-axis is *telling* and the y-axis is *doing*, and the resulting surface area of the square they create represents the potential for luck. The more you tell people about your passion, the further along the x-axis you travel, but if you don't pair that with hard work, you end up with a flattish rectangle with a small area. Similarly, if you put in loads of hard work but don't pair that with broadcasting your process, your surface area also isn't great.

You need both for the biggest possible surface area. Expertise *and* connections. Hard work *and* lucky breaks that come from others. Action *and* sharing and telling others about the actions you're taking. So, while we've seen time and again that taking action is what really moves the needle when it comes to bringing luck into your life, it needs to be an action that is shared, broadcast, and talked about.

Your luck will be directly proportional to the degree to which you actually do something about your passion, combined with the number of people you communicate this passion to.

"It's all hard work."
"It's about passion."
"It's not what you know; it's who you know."

It turns out that all of the above are true. Let's see how we can put this theory into practice and start bringing in the serendipity.

Step 1:
Think carefully about an area in life where you are trying to cultivate more luck, be it work or relationships or creative pursuits.

Step 2:
Draw a simple graph with *telling* on the x-axis and *doing* on the y-axis. Thinking about the past month, how much work did you do in this area of life? Imagine that on a scale of 1 to 10, that 10 is doing all you can to the best of your abilities. Similarly, ask yourself how often you've spoken to others about your project or goals, and to how many different people. Score 10 if you speak often and to more than a handful of people.

Step 3:
Draw the square and observe your total luck surface area. Now you can visually see if you are not doing enough of one or the other (or both!).

Step 4:
Based on what you find, commit to taking one step towards increasing this surface area. This could be by setting yourself the goal of talking to one new person per week about your passion, dedicating an extra hour every day to learning or building, or something in between.

Step 5:

Don't stop there! Pay close attention to the results these actions produce. Notice what works and, you guessed it, do more of that!

You may discover that you score low on *both* doing and telling. In this case, lucky you! It means that any action you take to increase either quantity will improve your overall luck exposure. Should you find that your surface area is actually pretty good already, then simply imagine a third dimension of time, and trust that if you keep going as you are, consistency and persistence will pay off.

As you consider the actions you'll take and the way you'll share your message, bear in mind what we've covered in previous chapters about a lucky mindset and thought patterns. Be resilient and patient, stay optimistic and don't get too neurotic about anything. Let's look at some examples.

You're looking for a new job but aren't having any luck. You follow the above process to check in on your luck surface area. You discover that while you're putting in hours submitting resumes, doing interviews and chatting to recruiters, you actually are spending barely any time just talking to people about your mission. In fact, you realize that most of your social circle don't even know you're looking for a job. Oops!

You take action. You go on social media to let everyone know who you are, and what you're looking for. You even ask close friends to ask around for you and see if anyone knows anyone looking for someone like you. These so-called "weak connections" (i.e. friends of friends of friends) are sometimes the most valuable in generating luck. Your friend's mom knows a guy whose wife teaches a course in the field you're trying to find work in. It's a long shot, but a few careful conversations and questions later, you get a mutual friend to introduce you. At first, you just approach her not looking for a job, but to ask her advice in general, and make a networking connection.

You have a nice chat, but she says she can't help you. However, she knows an ex student who started working for a company that was seemingly always hiring. She gives you their details. You reach out, mention her name, and get on a phone call with the director. He tells you they're not hiring, but he'll be in touch if anything comes up. A full month later, you finally hear from him – he doesn't want to hire you, but a colleague does, and are you interested?

You say yes, and "luckily" for you, you've got a million different versions of a brilliant resume on hand, so you can immediately jump in, prepared and ready for anything. You've been drilling interview questions for weeks, and not only that, you're also savvy about what other companies are offering salary-wise, since you've applied to so many positions. You ace the interview and within a few days you're hired for the perfect job for you.

Luck or hard work? This story would not have worked without either the hard work or the communication with others. The luck surface area theory explains how luck is a function of how proactive we are, and the relationships we're able to build with others.

Let's look at another example. Let's say you're trying to fulfil your lifelong dream of having a book published. You've had this dream since childhood, and everyone who knows you knows that this is your mission in life. But it occurs to you that there may be an imbalance between *doing* and *telling*.

While you tell everyone who will listen about your grand ideas for the book's structure, the ideas you want to share and why, when you sit down to draw the graph mapping out your luck surface area, you're surprised to see how little action you're actually taking towards this goal. In fact, the book is only half written and you haven't added to it in months. You already know that lucky breaks happen to those who boldly share their dreams and broadcast their goals, but you may have taken things too far, because you realize that you haven't written a book yet!

You realize you need a concrete action plan, so you commit to taking steps to write every day. You set a goal (let's say 1000 words), and when you speak to people, you're sure to tell them about what you're doing, and what progress you've made. From their point of view, you're not just talking excitedly anymore – you're doing something.

Finally, consider an example where the doing and the telling are both low. Perhaps it's time to admit to yourself if you are quietly harboring a dream that you've never told anyone about, *and* you've never taken any steps to realize. Maybe you're a proponent of the law of attraction and are still quietly hoping that wanting good things hard enough will somehow make them happen. Or maybe you lack faith and confidence in yourself, and your lack of luck in this area is a manifestation of the fact that you're not yet completely committed to this goal.

The luck surface area exercise is not meant to make you feel bad for what you're not doing, or not doing enough of. It's meant to help you identify those places in life that will most reward you if you pour your energy into them. What a shame to waste energy and time on things that will only yield a small result, if anything.

If there is not enough doing, then find a way, *today*, to take action:

- Set a small goal in the right direction, and then accomplish it.
- Create or build something, for example, write a chapter, make a business plan or work on your website.
- Learn something. Ask yourself what lack of knowledge is currently getting in the way, and commit to figuring out more about that area.

- Get organized. Tidy up your office, create a new filing system to keep track of documents, or plan your month ahead in detail.
- Solve problems. Ask for help, get rid of what isn't working, and strategize so that obstacles feel a little smaller going forward.

If there's not enough telling, then find a way, *today*, to start speaking up about your passion:

- If you introduce yourself to someone new, share a few details about what you're working on, and allow your excitement to show. Brag a little if you want to!
- Deliberately ask others to hold you accountable, or partner up with people who have projects of their own so you can regularly touch base and compare notes.
- Tell people whom you don't even necessarily think can help you in any way – you never know!
- Share your plans with people you admire and respect. This will give shape and definition to your goals, as well as motivate you to achieve your goals. Plus, these are the people most

likely to have insights or opportunities for you.
- Don't just share your triumphs. If you're having difficulties, speak up. Help and solutions may come specifically because you asked for them.
- Ask for advice and insight from others as a way to share your mission.

The surface area theory is all about the *interaction* between telling and doing, so, as best as you can, try to make your telling support your doing, and your doing support your telling. Make connections with new people, and then take actions that nurture that new relationship. Work hard and then share the results of that effort with others. Tell people what fires you up and why, and when they show an interest, be ready to run with it, and convert it to action.

Task 3: Visualize and repeat affirmations

The third method we're going to put under the microscope is the visualization and affirmation method. These two distinct but related techniques can be powerful tools towards building a lucky and more fortuitous life.

Visualization entails thinking about the goals we want to accomplish or the things we want to attain in our lives and using our imagination to generate an image of those things in our minds. There is no discrimination about what types of good fortune you can visualize having — physical, emotional, mental, and spiritual are all fair game. The key to good visualization is vividness – you want to conjure up an image that is as detailed and rich as possible. You can do this not only by drawing on all 5 of your senses but by remembering to include thoughts and emotions in the images you're visualizing.

You might, for example, visualize yourself being in the best physical shape of your life, parking your Land Rover in the garage of your mansion, or being welcomed home by your ideal spouse and adoring children as you walk through the door. Another version of this is to create what's known as a vision board, where you put a picture of everything you want to achieve or attain on a whiteboard so you can see it daily.

What's key in visualizing is to form as detailed a mental image as possible of what you want to achieve or attain. It may take time. You'd be surprised how often people think they know what they want, right up until they try to visualize it, and realize that they're unclear on the details or, once they immerse themselves in the vision, they see that it's not quite what they wanted. Visualizing makes things happen, but it helps you find clarity and focus on your goals.

The second part of this technique is to repeat positive affirmations about your goals and desires as you maintain the mental image of yourself having achieved and acquired these things in your mind. In other words, you are repeating to yourself phrases about what you want to accomplish and attain. The positive affirmations are repeated frequently — often in front of the mirror —to manifest whatever sort of positive energy is required for these visualizations to become a reality. For instance, you would look in the mirror and repeat, "I will be rich and own a large house" 10 times each morning.

Sound useless? Obviously, if you visualize outlandish and impossible things, no amount of positive affirmation will make those things come true. And the person who does precisely nothing to help that dream along is doing little more than indulging in fantasy. The real question is — in reasonable scenarios — does the visualization and affirmation method actually succeed in creating more desirable outcomes that are associated with luck? These are extremely popular methods to increase self-confidence, feelings of luck, and to extract what you want from life. But do they work? At first glance, the general idea is to increase your alertness and awareness of your goals. You are clearer on what you want, and may see in more detail the steps to get you there. But does visualizing and saying affirmations in itself make you more likely to achieve success and luck than someone who doesn't?

Allen Richardson, an Australian psychologist, attempted to measure the impact of positive mental visualization in a tangible way. He first had all of the study participants shoot free throws (basketball shots), recording data on each player to determine their baseline shooting ability. Richardson then separated the participants into groups:

- Group A - Practiced free throws every day for 20 days
- Group B - Only shot free throws on the first and last days of the study
- Group C - Only shot free throws on the first and last days of the study, but mentally

rehearsed shooting the free throws for 20 minutes per day every day in between

On the 20th day, all participants were gathered again and asked to shoot free throws.

Group A's shooting percentage increased by an average of 25% with the 20 days of practice. Group B, unsurprisingly, didn't show any improvement from their performances on the first day.

The discovery of the experiment, though, was that Group C's shooting percentage increased by an average of 24%, almost identical to Group A. This occurred despite the fact that Group A had physically practiced shooting free throws for 20 days, while Group C hadn't actually touched a basketball since the first day of the study.

Exciting result, right? Richardson concluded that positive visualization is indeed a powerful tool to be successful, at least in the case of putting a ball into a hoop. The participants who imagined the ball leaving their hands and traveling on a perfect trajectory until they watched it swish through the net showed truly remarkable improvement in 20 days. It is reasonable to say that they indeed made themselves more effective through positive visualization.

It might even be reasonable to say that one can make themselves luckier through visualizing the outcomes they want. The act of mental rehearsal can make you readier, more open, more aware, and more willing to jump into situations you might not have otherwise. It's as though your unconscious mind sets about finding ways to make the picture real, looking for solutions, noticing opportunities, and interpreting events according to that powerful vision held by the imagination. You might find yourself getting better and more opportunities if you visualize them happening. Sounds like luck to me.

Meanwhile, researchers at Carnegie Mellon University attempted to determine if self-affirmations could positively impact performance.

The researchers gathered a group of 73 college students and asked them to rank 11 personal values in order of importance to them. Half of the participants were given an exercise of self-affirmation in which they wrote about what made the values at the tops of their lists so important to them. The other half served as the control group, so they were asked to write about the value they had put ninth on their list.

To measure the effects of the self-affirmations on the participants, they were given a timed problem-solving test and intentionally subjected to stress by an evaluator. The results of the tests showed that the test-takers who had been a part of the self-affirmation group scored better on the test than those from the control group.

These results indicated that self-affirmations can be a beneficial tool that people can use to remain calm and think flexibly while under pressure. When we feel stressed and anxious, our brains typically can't operate as smoothly as we'd like. As stress is an undesirable reaction of our mind to stimulation, it's possible that positive self-affirmations can be helpful to anybody who experiences significant pressure to perform in work or school. Affirmations may not expressly help you perform better in themselves, but they'll help you *not perform poorly,* which is just as important most of the time.

This likely isn't the first time that you've heard about positive visualizations and affirmations, so it's good to know that this method actually does have some scientific merit behind it. We've seen that performance can be enhanced somewhat and that affirmations definitely have a positive effect on mood and anxiety. But the major question remains: Does the visualization and affirmation method legitimately increase your luck?

Kind of, yes.

That's as concrete of an answer as exists. The results of these studies do show that it is possible to positively influence our own mental states. That can definitely be characterized as setting the ground for luck, though not generating luck itself.

More importantly, these studies illustrate the power of believing in ourselves — not that we are lucky, but that we are capable. These methods — when applied reasonably — are in a way teaching us to shift to a more internal locus of control, where the role of luck is far less significant in our perceptions about the world and our abilities. Again, we run into the quandary of personal accountability denying the concept of luck. Again it would seem that the luckiest people are those that deliberately do not rely on luck but who instead embrace their agency and do what they can to bring about the results they want.

What about superstitions?

While many people consider themselves spiritual or religious, few among us would openly admit they believe in the more outlandish supernatural.

People might not willingly admit they believe in ghosts and monsters under the bed, but nonetheless, the vast majority of people have been shown to possess some sort of superstitious routines, have experienced an inexplicable hallucination, or have seen things they can only explain as *magic*. This has nothing to do with intelligence but rather something that all human beings naturally do –our evolved tendency to seek out patterns and cause-effect relationships.

Want your favorite sports team to win? You might just feel better if you wear the same pair of socks you wore the last time they won. It might be useless... but what if it's not? These things creep into our lives in small, almost imperceptible ways that make it second nature for us to believe in them.

Essentially, *the supernatural* has become a catch-all umbrella term for things that lack a conventional explanation. Can't explain it? It must be something supernatural. There may not always be a clear explanation, but blaming the missing cookies on a ghost and not the dog belies a very interesting tendency for humans to try to apply understanding to that which is out of their grasp.

You've likely read about this tendency when learning about ancient and not-so-ancient civilizations. The Greeks assigned a god to nearly everything as a scapegoat or savior while Native Americans engaged in rain dances to help their crops flourish for the coming harvest. We have the overwhelming desire to feel in control; if we are out of control, we risk feeling insignificant or subject to danger. When we feel we have control over something, we are suddenly more engaged and invested; if we feel there is no control, we feel helpless to the powers that be.

We believe in supernatural forces exerting control because something we don't understand, yet can blame, is far more comforting than no explanation at all. Humans just don't like to feel that we are random molecules of carbon and hydrogen that happened to coalesce and form somehow — we might be, but it sure feels better if we have a purpose.

This leads us to the question of superstitions, which are arguably the first way human beings developed to put their faith in the unexplained and supernatural.

Specifically, superstitions are behaviors or thought patterns that people engage in because they are hypothesizing the existence of a cause-and-effect relationship. You engage in superstitious acts because you believe it will get you closer to a specific outcome. For instance, if you notice that your favorite football team has won the past three times you've worn red underwear, a new superstition will be born: red underwear only on game days. You might not affect the game itself, but it appears that there is nevertheless a pattern of causation, so you're going to adhere to it — sometimes even subconsciously.

Classical conditioning is the cause for many superstitions we hold throughout our lives. We commit an act, we see an outcome, and we begin to link the two, even though it's no more than a correlation or simple coincidence. Surprisingly to some sports fans, sitting in the same chair while watching matches likely does not affect the end outcome just because it happened twice three years ago. This is why people don't walk under ladders— because negative occurrences have coincided with that event — never mind the fact that walking under a ladder puts you directly into the path of falling debris. A superstition, then, takes the place of a rule or law in a phenomenon we lack insight or understanding for.

Superstitious beliefs are what humans have a tendency to cling to — but it turns out, so do pigeons, as the famous psychologist B.F. Skinner proved in 1948. During his study, he found pigeons learned to continue behaviors that coincided with food appearing, despite the food appearing at set intervals, or even at random, intermittent intervals. In other words, pigeons saw patterns that produced an outcome they wanted and kept doing it, even though there was no causal relationship. The reason these superstitions developed was because of this absence of understanding of the real causes of events in the world.

Shana Wilson from Kent State University investigated why people, specifically sports fans, engage in superstitious behavior. They concluded that people who engage in superstitious behaviors are more susceptible to what is called the *uncertainty hypothesis*, which is the idea that when people experience a complete lack of certainty, they seek to find a way in which they can exert some degree of control over it. A lack of certainty is extremely uncomfortable, and being able to point to something as a cause eases the underlying tension.

We can find examples of this in our own daily lives. We all hate bumper-to-bumper traffic. We enjoy driving unimpeded to our destinations. Which would you prefer: bumper to bumper traffic, or driving unimpeded, both of which would culminate in you driving the same distance over the same amount of time? Most of us would choose the latter; we would choose to drive unimpeded because we can control the speed of our car and how slowly or quickly we go. To be stuck in a situation like bumper-to-bumper traffic where we have zero control and are subject to the infernal gods of traffic — that gives us feelings of hopelessness and helplessness.

Not having control over situations, at the extreme end of the spectrum, is a feeling which underlies certain types of anxiety and depression. What motivation could you possibly have if you were certain everything would turn out terribly, despite your efforts? Therefore, many times, the more important an uncontrollable situation is, the more likely people are to try to exert a measure of control over it through superstitious behavior. Here, we are seeing the shadow side of the internal/external locus of control idea. Taking control of our lives leads us to feeling happier – whether that control is real or only imagined.

Daniel Wann (2013) discovered that sports fans felt they could influence outcomes of games and matches with their superstitious behaviors, which typically involved clothing, food and drink, and good luck charms. Sports fan or not, the more you feel that your life is determined by factors outside your control, this research would argue, the more likely you'll become superstitious.

Superstitions are generally harmless unless they replace actual work and effort. If they do nothing to change the actual outcome of an event but make people feel better along the way, it's hard to see an issue. Problems arise when people can't distinguish between an outcome they can control and an outcome beyond their control. Stuart Vyse, author and professor at Connecticut College, chalks superstitious behaviors up to the comforts of illusory control, saying, "There is evidence that positive, luck-enhancing superstitions provide a psychological benefit that can improve skilled performance. There is anxiety associated with the kinds of events that bring out superstition. The absence of control over an important outcome creates anxiety. So, even when we know on a rational level that there is no magic, superstitions can be maintained by their emotional benefit. Furthermore, once you know that a superstition applies, people don't want to tempt fate by not employing it."

Positive superstitions can improve confidence and reduce anxiety because they are the panacea to all that ails you. If you are shy about a job interview and you always wear lucky socks during job interviews, you are going in with a head full of confidence because you feel you are complete and fully armored for battle. This is positive and can be helpful in providing a psychological advantage over not having any superstitious behaviors at all. As we explored in previous chapters, it's not the lucky socks so much as the way the lucky socks make us feel. These help us complete the self-fulfilling prophecy where if we think that we are (because of a superstitious behavior, anyway), then we are.

It's the same belief that can make us proclaim, "The talent was in you all along!" It's also in the powerful placebo effects that have stymied researchers the world over. When people believe there is a chance their actions are having an effect, they can convince themselves this effect has occurred – to the extent of actually bringing about that event.

So, should you partake in superstitions? Yes! But understand what they are and how they work. Superstitions are extremely easy to acquire, and they are likely more widespread than you realize. Our brains are fooling us into a sense of illusory control because it feels more comfortable that way. However, that comfort can distort reality in detrimental ways, or beneficial ways, depending on how we use them.

Takeaways:

- Our luck comes in part from our behaviors and choices, and those in turn come from our mindset and the way we think.

- If luck = preparation + opportunity, and we cannot control what opportunities come our way, then it means the only way to improve our luck is to focus on being prepared to strike when a lucky chance does come our way.
- An obvious way to bring more luck to your life is to work hard, even if the results are far off or not guaranteed.
- Hard work isn't all that matters, though. The surface area theory of luck explains that our luck is a result of both *doing* and *telling*, i.e., hard work combined with how ready we are to talk about our passion with others. You can construct your own doing/telling graph to determine where you need to put your efforts to increase your luck.
- We can also increase luck by using the methods of visualization and positive affirmations. Both have been shown scientifically to improve performance and lead to better outcomes. To work well, visualizations have to be rich and vivid, and affirmations have to be said regularly. Naturally, both work best when paired with concrete action taken towards your goals!
- Superstitious behaviors are a human tendency that evolved in the face of

uncertainty, as a way to feel in control. There is no magic, but belief in the power of a superstition can be powerful in itself. The best superstitions, however, are those that encourage an internal locus of control and which don't distort our perception of what is and isn't under our control.

Chapter 5. Coincidence and Serendipity

There are two phenomena that humans commonly associate with luck — coincidence and serendipity.

Serendipity is the occurrence and development of favorable or beneficial events, seemingly by chance. It's finding on the ground the exact amount of money you later discover you're short at a restaurant. It's a book falling open at precisely the chapter that you most need in your research project, and which you've been wondering about for ages. Serendipity is meeting somebody who grew up in the same small town as you while you are both living in an urban metropolis on the other side of the country. Whenever you find yourself saying, "It's a small world" or "wow, what are the chances?" you've probably experienced some serendipity.

Similarly, a coincidence is a remarkable concurrence of events or circumstances with seemingly no casual connection to one another. The word 'coincidence' can be used affirmatively, as in, "It is a crazy coincidence that we wore the same colored shirts as each other three days in a row." However, it is also common to use "coincidence" in the negative, such as, "It can't be a coincidence that we wore the same colored shirts as each other three days in a row." It can also be positive or negative, respectively: "I can't believe we are both from the same village of under 500 inhabitants" or "I can't believe my ex-boyfriend is here out of all the restaurants in this huge city."

While random chance is an inherent part of both phenomena, the more of each we experience personally, the luckier we appear to be. Some have devised elaborate theories to explain these seemingly magical experiences, from Jung's theory of synchronicity to those who would believe guardian angels are pulling the strings for us behind the scenes. What we really want to know, though, is whether or not these seemingly random events are actually connected somehow, or if they are truly just a result of statistical probabilities. Are there explanations for what we might perceive as luck, coincidence, and serendipity? And if so, is there a way to bring about more of them?

The "Serendipity Mindset"

What we've been calling luck till now could also be termed serendipity. This is like a chance encounter with randomness that leaves us feeling charmed and favored. Many people credit serendipity and coincidence with finding a dream job, meeting the love of their life or narrowly avoiding disaster and finding their lives saved. As we've seen, even things like major scientific breakthroughs occur as a result of a serendipitous accident. Things like Velcro, penicillin and microwave ovens are all inventions that required a little serendipity. In fact, the field of combinatorial chemistry is all about using accidental combinations to generate new and potentially useful compounds.

Just as we can court and nurture lucky opportunities, as well as be ready to strike when they appear, we can also make it more likely that serendipity falls into our laps. Connecting the dots this way is again, as you can probably guess, about mindset.

Serendipity comes from the unknown – so it makes sense that our attitude towards the unexpected largely shapes our relationship with it and how much luck we experience.

We cannot create the unexpected, by definition, but we can create ideal conditions for the unexpected to thrive and take shape. Christian Busch, PhD is the author of the book *The Serendipity Mindset*, where he explores the role we have in cultivating the elements of a lucky, serendipitous life.

According to Busch, serendipity is made of 3 key ingredients:

The **Trigger**. This is when something unexpected or out of the ordinary happens. The trigger is a stimulus that is surprising, unusual, and somehow meaningful to you.

The **Connection**. Serendipity is about seemingly random connections and relationships. Still, we can create a link between the trigger and something else in our lives that, on the surface, seems unrelated to the trigger.

The **Value**. This is where the magic happens. We take the connection we've made and find in it a possible solution, a new insight into the situation, or a novel avenue to explore further.

As you can see, the above is about noticing what little threads and emergent surprises are happening in our world, and engaging with them actively. This means taking action but leaving plenty of room for things to evolve spontaneously, usually in ways we can't predict or even understand. Sometimes, these steps will play out all on their own, but we can also take a more "half-formed" moment of serendipity and bring it to fruition by noticing it and capitalizing on it deliberately. It's all about creating a life when serendipity is allowed to bubble up and where we ourselves are free to link up the dots when we see them. There may be countless opportunities flying by without our proactive effort right under our noses!

Some examples will show that this works in the real world.

Imagine you're at a party and meeting a few new people. They ask what work you do, and you (remembering the surface area luck theory) excitedly say that you're an adult education teacher, but you're currently launching a new mental health program where you partner with recent graduates from the counselling course at your college. The other person says, "Oh, cool! My aunt used to do something like that, I think. She was an art teacher, but she was part of this foundation that did all sorts of things with community counseling, too."

Now, you could easily let this little spark of connection fly by and never think of it again. After all, you don't care about teaching art, and your college doesn't even offer it. You could start talking about something else or end the conversation. But with a Serendipity mindset, you decide to grasp the trigger and make a connection. What is similar between what you've been told and what you're doing in your own life currently? Quite a lot in this case.

You mention that you're having some trouble launching because of a lack of premises to set anything up, and you're unsure about a few legalities involved. How did this person's aunt get around it? Can she tell you more? A few minutes into the conversation, you have sowed a seed. Perhaps in a week, they come back to you with a nice bit of luck – the aunt shares some information about a grant you can apply for that you knew nothing about previously – a grant that turns out to be exactly what you needed to get going in your project.

This little encounter might not seem like much, but with just a few tweaks to mindset, moments like these can make a world of difference to your life. Granted, there is nothing anyone can do to make sure that just the right person shows up at a party that day, and that you talk to them. But as we've seen, even in this regard, we can do things to help by increasing our exposure to luck and getting out there to talk to people, say yes to opportunities and generally get curious about the world.

If you pair this with a proactive, positive and curious mindset, you become a better conversationalist who listens and pays attention to potential triggers coming your way (rather than blabbing on about yourself, or getting bogged down in negativity). Because you're open-minded, relaxed and curious, people share things with you and find your attitude infectious.

Something else to consider is that understanding the elements of luck can help you maximize serendipity, but you can also help by creating your own triggers. If someone at a party asks what you do, and you say, "I'm a teacher," and leave it at that, you might completely miss out on a whole thread of opportunity. You never hear about the aunt. You never hear about the grant you could have applied for. The chance was always there – but you needed to be oriented in just the right way to "catch" it. Share details with people – you never know which one might be a trigger to follow somewhere interesting!

Luckily, getting good at sniffing out serendipity triggers is not all that different from being a good conversationist in general. It requires we proactively engage with others and open ourselves to letting the conversation evolve in unexpected and unplanned ways. It means listening properly to actually hear what you're told, and allowing yourself to have preconceived ideas or beliefs challenged. A sense of humor, kindness, and a problem-solving attitude allow us to be active but not crush any emerging opportunity that doesn't look quite like what anyone imagined.

Questions are great at keeping you open-minded, but be aware that the way you ask questions can shut down possibility. If you define your challenge and scope of possibility too early on, you close yourself off to emergent solutions you didn't imagine previously. For example, if you go into a conversation with the foregone question, "How do I secure a venue for this project," you are closing yourself off to the possibility of an unrelated solution, i.e., not in a venue but in a grant you hadn't considered. It goes without saying that questions like, "what's wrong with me that I can't figure this out?" shut you off to solutions even further!

When you ask people questions, keep it open-ended. What are your thoughts? Any ideas? Of course, a big part of this is conveying a sense that you are actually listening to and care about the answers you're given. Everyone knows how frustrating it is, for example in a work context, where "brainstorming" is just a box ticking exercise, and everyone knows that the boss has already decided what they're going to do. Keep optimistic and *believe* that there are solutions and opportunities out there; you just have to find them.

- See other people as co-creators in your vision, and goldmines for valuable insights, new ideas and fresh perspectives. Share your story and get curious about theirs. If you can identify those "super connectors" in your social ecosystem, all the better.

- Don't compartmentalize areas of your life in separate boxes. You might get a fantastic business idea while on vacation, or have an insight from work to bring to your family life. The more distant and novel the connection, the potentially more powerful.
- No coincidence is too small. If you notice something, or a connection is forming in your mind, explore it. Speak up about it. "I know this may sound crazy, but have you ever thought about…?"
- Look at problems in your world and ask how they could be reframed as opportunities. A restaurateur has a power outage one night, and the following night, he has a conversation with a blind person who tells them they're a supertaster. He puts the two together: why not have an "in the dark" restaurant where people can focus on the food while the lights are out?
- Give yourself time every day for undirected, unstructured time where you just experience life and sink into aware observation. See what pops up in your own mind when you aren't rushing from one thing to the next. See

what you notice when you pause for a while and just observe what's in front of you without any preconceptions.
- Be suspicious of conformity, easy answers and fixed ideas. Let go of the desire to control and notice not what is failing to happen according to plan but what is actually emerging. This is how Viagra was discovered – while testing the medicine for another purpose, a surprising side effect emerged. The successful medicine would not exist now if the researchers had fixated on what it wasn't doing, instead of what it was!
- In conversations, don't be afraid to come right out and ask, "so what is inspiring you right now?" or "what are your current challenges?" to cut to the chase.
- Get creative and mix things up. What would happen if you mixed two seemingly unrelated ideas, or completely deconstructed a story you had so you could rewrite it in a different order? Sometimes, all that's needed to welcome fresh change is a shift in perspective. Have you ever noticed how often an "aha!" moment comes from simply being in an odd

position – upside down, in a hotel bath, walking in a strange new city? If you're stuck on a problem, go to a completely new café and think about it there for a while.
- Finally, don't be in a rush to resolve ambiguity. Keep things open, and be relaxed and playful with what is unknown or tricky to nail down. Give opportunity seedlings time to grow and sprout.

Most people loathe the idea of networking or cheesy self-promotion, whether that's in the business world or in dating. But simply meeting people is not enough – there is an art to making those connections fruitful for you. Don't get discouraged if the hunt for serendipity doesn't yield much at first. Be patient and let things incubate, Have faith in weak connections and invisible links set in motion.

Remember that your perspective today can reframe yesterday's flop as today's serendipity. Be resilient and keep it up. Serendipity will not thrive in an atmosphere of judgment, shame or foregone conclusions. Instead, let yourself make mistakes and play, relishing the wonder and joy you create when you let go of outcomes and focus instead on the process.

Someone walks into a crowded restaurant and sees there are no tables. Instead of leaving, on a whim they ask to sit at an empty seat at someone else's table. They notice that this person is reading a book – they aren't shy and speak up, sharing how they went to school with the author. This starts a conversation that ends up in the two being married two years later. It's hard to imagine this moment of serendipity happening without the first person's optimistic, easy-going and open-ended attitude, as well as their willingness to speak to a stranger. How many such opportunities are around us all the time, just one small choice or question away from being realized?

Serendipity

We can consider serendipity to be the combination of two main factors — *seemingly improbable occurrences and positive personal feelings about them*. Unexpectedly running into an old friend is serendipitous, especially because it might lead to a profitable professional relationship, a rekindled romance, or even just sharing an enjoyable meal. On the other hand, when you just as unexpectedly run into an old nemesis and are reminded why you disliked them in the first place — well, that's not serendipitous in the slightest. You need the positive feelings associated for it to be considered *good* luck and not just an accident.

Stephen Makri is a prominent lecturer in the field of information interaction at City University London. He's conducted several studies with the intention of better understanding what serendipity is, and the different ways people perceive it in their own lives.

In a study published in 2014, Makri questioned professionals in creative fields about what they do personally to increase their likelihood of experiencing a serendipitous encounter. Most of their answers related to variability in some way or another — mixing things up at the office by working in different environments with different people, or just generally being aware of getting bogged down in an overly repetitive routine so that they can try to change things up more frequently.

Makri summed up his thoughts on the results of his studies and the relationship between luck and serendipity by saying: "I think that luck means different things to different people — some people use it as a synonym for serendipity. But others were clear that the two were different — luck was totally out of our control and there's nothing that we can do to influence it. They think that serendipity can't be controlled but it could be influenced."

One of the interesting things about serendipity or other fortuitous events is that we often don't realize just how beneficial they are until long after the fact. Sometimes, the only thing that distinguishes bad luck from good luck is the passage of time. Reminiscing on a lucky event in the past might lead us to an understanding or insight of how it served as a catalyst to create positive change for us. It can sometimes be rewarding, or perhaps even unsettling, to reflect on cause and effect in our own lives, and to realize how small and seemingly innocuous occurrences of the past have had massive impacts on our current selves. One more reason to be grateful and optimistic in your interpretations!

Let's say that you usually eat lunch at your office, but one day you decide to go buy a sandwich from a local deli. You see an old friend from high school, Mary, as you're waiting in line. You and Mary make the usual small-talk while catching up, and when you tell Mary you're working as a graphic designer, she says that she has another friend in the business she could connect you with. You say that you would appreciate that, exchange information, and go separate ways.

In a vacuum, the significance of this interaction is rather ambiguous, and calling it serendipitous would seem premature unless catching up with Mary was the most exciting thing to happen all day.

Now imagine that you and Mary weren't that close, and re-establishing a relationship with her isn't really worth the effort to you. You never follow up with her, and this is the end of the tale.

But what if, instead, you've been struggling to add new clients online, and you simply can't pass up the networking opportunity. So, you follow up with Mary and get in touch with her friend. Mary's recommendation starts you off on the right foot, and from there, you develop a business partnership and friendship with *her* friend that lasts for years.

Suppose you hadn't chosen to eat at the deli instead of in your office like usual. In that case, you might never have run into Mary, connected with her friend, and benefited both professionally and personally for years as a result. Suddenly, this is one of the most serendipitous events of your life. It started with you not being closed off to the idea of trying something new (the deli) and also not writing Mary off just because she personally wasn't very relevant to you at that moment.

The real difference between status quo and serendipity, however, was in the effort you put in *afterward*. There's your chance to go in and extract value from random connections, and make them mean something. Being open, positive, and proactive makes people more likely to recognize and appreciate an opportunity so that they will take advantage of the potential good fortune they receive.

In reality, serendipitous events are simply good things that have a low probability of occurring. As such, we can increase our chances of serendipity just by putting ourselves in situations where — however improbable — good things can happen to us. You're not going to have a moment of serendipity at home watching television, but just walking outside raises the probability one notch higher. Going to a social event with somebody you don't hang out with often will bump it up again. Doing new things with different people constantly will all but guarantee a steady flow of opportunities that could be seen as serendipitous in hindsight. There's also a case to be made for simply doing what you'd normally do, but in an unfamiliar way – when you're out of your dally rut, *you* are different, and people respond to you differently.

Of course, the opposite is true as well. Bad luck is far more likely to fall upon you when you are constantly doing new things with different people than if you stayed at home safe and sound. But on the other hand, a lucky chain reaction may well begin with something that seems unfortunate on the surface. So it's a reasonable conclusion that our *perceptions* about reality, and luck specifically, are important factors in how lucky or unlucky we end up being.

Coincidence

When you want to encompass the full spectrum of improbable occurrences that happen in our lives — from serendipitous to terribly misfortunate — you call them coincidences. All serendipity is a coincidence by virtue of it occurring despite having a low probability that it would, but not all coincidences are serendipitous, unfortunately.

There are two sides to the "I don't believe in coincidences" coin, however. On one side, there are the people who believe that all coincidences are really just signs with a deeper meaning — whether it's coming from the universe or some other force — pointing them toward some sort of personal enlightenment or enrichment. On the other side of the coin are those who say that believing in coincidences is a result of a lack of understanding about statistical probabilities.

In 1989, mathematicians Persi Diaconis and Frederick Mosteller published a paper titled *Methods for Studying Coincidences*. At first, they considered a broad definition of the term as encompassing all rare events but eventually settled on the definition: "A coincidence is a surprising concurrence of events, perceived as meaningfully related, with no apparent casual connection."

Interestingly, coincidences shouldn't be that surprising from a statistical point of view because they happen all the time. As statistician David Hand put it humorously in his book, *The Improbability Principle,* "Extremely improbable events are commonplace."

What makes them seem crazy, strange, or extraordinary then? What makes us lose our minds over them and proclaim great or terrible luck? The answer is that mostly, we stink at calculating probabilities.

Our brains are in some ways just like computers — processing information as efficiently as they can and conserving as much energy as possible. But given our processing rate and all of the complexities of cause and effect, it is inefficient or even impossible for us to objectively calculate probabilities as we go about our daily lives. Remember that your brain is a pattern-seeking and meaning-making machine – and it has evolved to do those things very quickly. We can estimate, but our accuracy is not likely to be particularly noteworthy.

Add in the fact that there are now over 7.5 billion people globally, and the opportunities for statistical improbabilities to occur are everywhere. Throw in the internet and the power for social media to bring any two elements together, and the picture gets more and more interesting. Diaconis and Mosteller's *Law of Truly Large Numbers* states, "With a large enough sample, any outrageous thing is likely to happen." The odds that your one lottery ticket will win the Powerball are infinitesimally small, but the odds that somebody's —anybody's — ticket will win it are actually considerable. The winner will feel they have been blessed with incredibly good fortune, but the buyers of the millions of tickets that win nothing likely won't think twice about it — after all, they didn't have a high probability to win in the first place.

This also harkens back to the classic example of probability — if you were to put an infinite number of monkeys into a room with typewriters and wait for an infinite amount of time, it is a statistical eventuality that one of them would bang out a perfect recreation of Shakespeare's *Romeo and Juliet*.

When you begin to look at coincidences as low probabilities, it actually begins to seem inevitable that you'll experience some from time to time. When you think about all of the people you know and all the places you go, and then consider all of the places that all of the people you know are going — chances are good that you'll bump into somebody you know, somewhere, at some point. For instance, if you live in the same city as someone, are near the same age, have overlapping friends and interests, and have similar diets, there really aren't so many places you would both spend time.

The 49 times that we go to the grocery store, shop, and check out without seeing any friends or acquaintances don't register, but that one time that you see an old teacher from a class you were in over a decade ago is probably going to give your brain a big jolt of nostalgia, thus highlighting the coincidence.

And those are just the coincidences that are actually realized. How many near-coincidences have you learned about after the fact? You might be talking to a friend and find out that you randomly ate lunch at the same restaurant on the same day, but sat on opposite sides of the restaurant and just didn't see each other. When you start to include the close calls, the probability of some coincidence occurring at some point suddenly seems even greater.

The further we examine these ideas, the more apparent it becomes that luck might just be an inaccurate way of describing our interaction with these external events and circumstances. We may not have enough information to do the math behind the cause and effect that creates our present reality, but we can still accept that it is there. And when we factor in our positive feelings about particular outcomes, it's not hard to see why we'd sometimes feel like there was a supernatural force looking out for us.

Psychiatrist and author of the book *Connecting with Coincidence,* Bernard Beitman, studied how various personality traits relate to views on coincidences. He found that people who describe themselves as religious, spiritual, or otherwise seeking a higher meaning in life have greater likelihoods of seeing coincidences in their lives. Likewise, self-referential (likely to relate external information to themselves) people are also prone to experience more coincidences. Coincidence, like luck, is a tool that humans use to make ourselves feel better when we feel sad, angry, or anxious by creating meaning from all the natural chaos around us.

According to Beitman, there are three categories of coincidences — environment-environment interactions, mind-environment interactions, and mind-mind interactions.

Environment-environment interactions are those coincidences that are objectively observable in the physical world. Your run into your high school sweetheart in a foreign city after not seeing each other in 10 years, which leads to a rekindled romance. These are the most obvious and easiest to understand of the coincidences.

Slightly less objective are the mind-environment interactions, where you randomly think about something or somebody, and then some event relating to that thing or person happens in your life. This might be thinking about a friend you haven't caught up with in months and then receiving a text from that friend later the same day. These premonition-esque coincidences might feel cool, but they are also highly difficult to measure.

The last category, mind-mind interactions, is uncommon and might seem mystical. Beitman coined the term "simulpathity" to describe a mind-mind interaction in which one person experiences the pain or emotion of somebody else who is far away. This is most frequently reported between twins, and while it is the least associable form of coincidence with luck, it is certainly an interesting phenomenon to ponder.

It can be difficult to change your perception about coincidences. Maybe you don't even want to because believing in them seems like a harmless thing people do to make themselves feel better. But in reality, understanding coincidences for what they are doesn't necessarily change the feelings those coincidences elicit in us. You can understand that running into an old friend in an unexpected place is statistically probable to happen every once in a while, yet still, be grateful and excited when it does happen.

Furthermore, thinking in terms of probabilities allows you to manipulate those probabilities in your favor, if you so choose, by constantly doing new things with new people in different places so you have more opportunities to experience low-probability occurrences. Clearly, this correlates with greater luck.

With that in mind, let's examine something referred to as the birthday paradox to better grasp the math behind our coincidences. Given a sample size of 23 people, there is a 50-50 chance that two people will have the same birthday. At first, this is counterintuitive. There are 365 days in a year, so how could such a small sample size create even odds? The reason this doesn't immediately compute is that our brains struggle to do computation with exponents.

With 23 people, there are 253 chances for a matching birthday. The first person has 22 people to compare with, the next has 21, and so on. Summing all of the numbers from 22 down to 1 gives us 253. Now the chance that any 2 people have *different* birthdays is 364/365 — this is the number in the back of your head, making the 50-50 odds so confusing. However, when we take the fraction 364/365 and raise it to the exponent 253, we get the result 0.4995, or approximately 50%.

Essentially, each of the 253 times that there is a chance for two people to have the same birthday, we are multiplying the fraction 364/365 by itself, reducing it ever so slightly and increasing the odds of two people out of the 23 having the same birthday.

We simply can't do this calculation in our heads, much like the probabilities of the vast majority of the coincidental and serendipitous occurrences of our lives. But whether we can do the calculations or not, the math is still there, governing the seemingly random occurrences of our lives. And, of course, it's easy to interpret much of this as fortuitous luck.

Takeaways:

- Coincidence and serendipity are related to good luck. We all would like something beneficial and fortuitous to happen to us for seemingly no good reason. We can't create positive random chances, but we can foster a "serendipity mindset" that helps us notice and take advantage of the chances that come our way.
- Serendipity means different things to different people, but generally, it is the combination of seemingly improbable occurrences plus positive personal feelings about them. We can cultivate a serendipity mindset by recognizing triggers in daily life, drawing connections

to other unrelated areas, and finding potential value in that link.
- Making use of the unexpected requires that we are optimistic, open-ended, comfortable with ambiguity, extraverted, and good listeners, as well as willing to make mistakes or entertain unexpected outcomes. We need to be proactive and curious about what emerges spontaneously.
- The real difference between the status quo and serendipity is in the effort you put in following a chance happening, and the meaning you can assign to events after the fact.
- Statistician David Hand claims that although coincidences seem surprising, "extremely improbable events are commonplace." It is only the limits of our human understanding of probability that makes coincidence seem more astonishing.
- Luck is a way of describing our interaction with random external events. Those who are religious or spiritual tend to experience more coincidences and perceive them differently. Similarly, self-referential people – i.e., those who tend to connect external events to themselves –

also describe more coincidence experiences.

Chapter 6. Wiseman's Four Factors

"You gotta ask yourself one question. 'Do I feel lucky?' Well, do ya, punk?"

Clint Eastwood's *Dirty Harry* famously asked this pivotal question in 1971, but it's a question as old and mysterious as time itself. Do I feel lucky? What makes me lucky? And what is luck, anyway? As we've seen, could it really be a *feeling* after all? Again, we end up at the laurels of British professor Richard Wiseman's studies and conclusions on kismet's role in our lives.

Over the course of ten years, Wiseman interviewed hundreds of people about the ways luck factored into their daily lives, and numerous patterns emerged. Eventually,

Wiseman detailed his conclusions in the book *The Luck Factor*, in which he reveals that while his subjects had almost no insights into the causes of their luck, they displayed consistent patterns of behavior that were directly responsible for their good or bad fortune.

We've covered some of these results earlier in the book, and this chapter builds on the narrative of certain traits and factors that typically accompany the presence of luck. Again, this isn't to say that doing X or Y literally *causes* you to win at Blackjack or meet that special someone, only that it makes some hidden, intermediate steps more possible. It's these steps that ultimately lead to fortunate outcomes.

Wiseman conducted many controlled experiments that allowed him to observe "luck" in action. In one experiment, he simply asked volunteers to walk up the street to a specific coffee shop and order a cup of coffee. Unbeknownst to his subjects, he had left money on the ground in their path and had positioned a well-connected businessman inside the shop. A young man who described himself as lucky discovered the money and pocketed it on his way to the shop, and randomly struck up a conversation with the businessman while waiting for his beverage.

A different volunteer, who self-described as unlucky, stepped right over the cash and kept to herself while at the coffee shop. By now, you can probably spot the behaviors and attitudes that led to such different outcomes when provided with roughly the same environmental stimuli in each case.

The vastly different experiences of the volunteers demonstrate Wiseman's notion that some personality types are luckier because they create scenarios that maximize opportunities, thereby increasing their luck. Attitude alone cannot change the fact of what's on the floor or who is in the coffee shop, but it sure does open you up to these details in a useful way.

Each volunteer was presented with identical opportunities, but their individual mindsets dictated their course of action. Had the unlucky woman widened her focus just a bit, she would have picked up the money and maybe enjoyed a free cup of coffee. But with her unlucky mindset, she didn't expect the unusual bonus, didn't look for it, and missed it completely. Likewise, her unwillingness to chat up a stranger while waiting for coffee could have cost her a valuable connection.

The primary difference between these two volunteers, says Wiseman, is that the "lucky" man was open to chance opportunities, thereby making him likelier to notice the unexpected in his environment. He wasn't actually any more fortunate or blessed than the unlucky person.

This openness, similar to the trait described in a previous chapter, is the first of four factors determining luck.

Be Open to New Experiences

Lucky people are open to new possibilities. This can be a tricky attitude to pin down, but such people tend to be somewhat relaxed about life, adopting the general attitude that everything is all right. Wiseman found that they have lower levels of anxiety than their unlucky counterparts, which frees them to not only expect good things, but to look for them actively. Think about what makes you anxious. At its basic level, anxiety is a question of control – feeling as though you don't have it, or as though you need to work hard to get it back. If you imagine that anxiety and attitude of control is a *narrowing of perception*, you can see that staying optimistically open-ended is a question of attention and awareness. The "unlucky" woman who walked past the money on the floor? Who knows what stressful ruminations she might have been distracted by at that moment, which caused her to figuratively close her eyes to the luck right in front of her?

According to the professor, unlucky people are frequently stuck in routines. These routines focus on the end goals versus the process or journey – and so they miss the journey, which is frequently where interesting new opportunities show up! They have a tendency to hyper-focus on accomplishing specific tasks, and as a result, they are blinded to other possibilities. The old saying, "If you do what you've always done, you'll get what you always get," is applicable here. It's as though we cling so tightly to what we think should happen, that we are unable to see what could happen, or what is happening that's actually *better*. Remaining within your comfort zone assures that new experiences are unlikely to come your way, and if they do, you are apt to miss them.

The takeaway here is to relax your focus and be open to unexpected possibilities. Anything can turn into something if you allow it to.

Listen to Your Gut

The second factor affecting luck is to listen to your intuition. Lucky people are more willing to take a risk by following their gut instinct – which they are able to listen to because they are more receptive, open0minded and relaxed about what is unfolding in the present moment.

However, it's not just about hunches and feelings – the willingness to take action may be the key. Unlucky people are usually reticent to act until they can prove the move is sound. They get stuck in research mode, or suffer from "analysis paralysis." Born of anxiety, analysis paralysis is the inability to act swiftly or decisively and to overthink ideas or situations, often passing up good opportunities in the process. Frequently, by the time a situation has been thoroughly examined, the window in which to has passed. And you're still anxious.

Wiseman suspects that our brains are wired in such a way that intuition represents a pattern detected by our body and brain, but that our conscious mind has not yet recognized. Our lifetime of experiences and interactions are stored in the pathways of the brain, and it identifies and responds to familiar stimuli much faster than we can perceive. Trusting a hunch frequently yields a greater benefit than creating an exhaustive list of pros and cons. Lucky people realize that if they have a strong gut feeling, it is often worth their time to stop and consider it. They've learnt not only to trust themselves, but also to not let the possibility of failure completely deter them from taking occasional risks. This is all to say that our gut hunches and intuition are far smarter than we realize, and by listening to them, we put ourselves in situations that turn out to be fortuitous and lucky.

Case in point: Apple co-founder Steve Jobs takes a calligraphy class.

On a whim, college dropout Jobs decided to take a calligraphy class, where he learned about serif and sans-serif fonts, varying the amount of space between letter combinations, and what makes beautiful typography an art form. The class had no practical application in his life until ten years later, when he was designing the first Macintosh computer. The Mac incorporated multiple typefaces and proportionally spaced fonts, revolutionary concepts that have since become industry standards.

Said Jobs, "Of course, it was impossible to connect the dots looking forward when I was in college. But it was very, very clear looking backwards ten years later. So, you have to trust that the dots will somehow connect in your future. You have to trust in something — your gut, destiny, life, karma, whatever. This approach has never let me down, and it has made all the difference in my life." You can imagine that from an anxious, control-prone mindset, a calligraphy class would have seemed like a stupid idea, and the fact that its usefulness only became relevant ten years down the line would have frustrated someone who was stressed and wanted innovative solutions *right now*.

He followed his instinct to learn about the elements of what makes a beautiful product, which eventually became Apple's hallmark and claim to business immortality – beautiful design and functionality. There may not have been an immediate payoff for Jobs' relative gamble, and he may not have even been fully conscious of his reasoning. But it showed that his vague inkling that elements of calligraphy would be central to his career was correct.

Positive Expectations

Lucky people are certain that their futures are full of good fortune. Rose-colored glasses are not just about being whimsical and unrealistic, though. Though lucky people tend to be optimistic and to hope for the best, this attitude gives lucky people more resilience and "grit," says Wiseman. In other words, when people hold the belief that things will work out, they are apt to persevere.

Perseverance in turn builds resilience, which allows a person to hold fast, giving more time for events to work out in their favor. Optimistic people look on the bright side no matter the outcome, and as a result, they have less anxiety and tend to discover unrealized opportunities in misfortune. They understand that they are capable of handling what life throws at them, and this confidence allows them to have a more relaxed attitude because suddenly, not every little thing is a life-or-death matter. When things don't go as expected, they don't throw their hands in the air and give up, interpreting the result as proof that that universe is out to get them somehow. Lucky people, instead, are the ones most likely to say, "when one door closes, another opens" – and believe it.

Finally, they are also more willing to reach out for help and support during times of crisis, which lowers their anxiety level and provides others with new opportunities to utilize their own life experiences and expertise. And as we saw earlier, reaching out to share your joys and tribulations helps you build valuable connections with others. Those relationships can be the very channels through which luck finds its way to you. Given the opening, people usually love to help, and these types of positive interactions benefit all the involved parties, once again increasing the luck factor.

That doesn't mean that lucky people don't experience setbacks — it just means that their attitude toward the outcome differs greatly from that of the unlucky. The experiences of Chuck Noland in the movie *Castaway* come to mind. As a successful Federal Express systems engineer, Chuck travels the world resolving productivity issues at FedEx terminals until his plane crashes in the Pacific Ocean. As the only survivor, Chuck is forced to adapt to life on a remote island for four years until being rescued.

Throughout the film, Chuck exhibits positive expectations despite his grim circumstances. He continually hopes for the best while demonstrating resilience in preparing for the worst. He learns how to spearfish for food and creates conveniences for himself from the FedEx cargo that washes up on the beach. He even fashions a buddy, Wilson, out of a volleyball, thus creating "human" interaction for himself and keeping a lively discussion of ideas and plans alive in the face of a bleak future.

Here, elements of hope, optimism, and the choice to be happy contribute to luck. It's no wonder many philosophers have named hope as the most important trait a person can possess.

Transform Bad Luck into Good

One specific technique employed by the character of Chuck Noland is "counterfactual thinking." According to psychologists, the degree to which you think that something is fortunate (or not) is the degree to which you imagine alternatives that are better (or worse). Again, it's a question of interpretation and perception.

In other words, lucky people always look for the silver lining. In Noland's case, he reasoned that he could have died in the plane crash, or been eaten by sharks. In his mind, he was *lucky* to have survived, even if that meant living alone on an island. Therefore, one of the key characteristics for transforming bad luck into good is the ability to face adversity and take control of the situation, not be buried by it. Trust that life has prepared you to handle whatever comes along. Or, if a situation is outside your experience, know that others can help and be willing to accept their support. Actively look for the unseen opportunity in misfortune.

Professor Wiseman gives this example: Unlucky people say, "I can't believe I've been in another car accident." Lucky people say, "Yes, I had a car accident, but I wasn't killed." The point is that both ways of thinking are unconscious and automatic. It would never occur to the unlucky people to see it a different way. This gives them the ability to keep on moving and adapt.

Make Your Own Luck

Examining Wiseman's four factors of luck, it is clear that mindset is the key factor.

The way you perceive the events of your life determines whether or not you feel lucky. Optimism, perseverance, and resilience are significant characteristics that differentiate good luck from bad. A relaxed, open attitude toward life is another contributing factor. Professor Wiseman notes, "Lucky people create, notice, and act upon the chance opportunities in their lives."

Create — notice — act. These qualities are the hallmarks of people with good luck. *Create* scenarios where you are interacting with and meeting new people. If activities like networking don't come naturally, attach yourself to someone who knows how to work a room, and ask them to include you. When someone mentions a topic that interests you, maximize the opportunity to talk with them about it. *Notice* the myriad opportunities that continually surround you. If you are frantic or stressed or goal-driven, learn how to slow down and relax to avoid missing the available prospects.

Make space in your busy brain for new experiences. *Act* quickly when your instinct sends you a strong signal. Pay attention, but not too hard. Don't overthink it — trust that your unconscious has detected a pattern and is urging you to make an effective, beneficial decision.

Professor Wiseman makes one final distinction — there is a difference between chance and luck. He reminds us that chance events are like winning the lottery. They are events over which we have no control other than buying a ticket. When people say that they consistently experience good fortune, he believes, it has to be because of something they are doing. We have far more control over events than we perceive. You might believe that 50% of life is due to chance events. It is not — perhaps 10% is attributed solely to chance. That other 40% you think you have no influence over at all is actually defined by the way you think, embodied in these four factors and traits. Imagine what your life would look like if it was 40% luckier.

How to strengthen the four factors

In the following chapter, we're going to take a closer look at concrete steps to hack your way to better luck, but first, let's explore some ways to bring a little of Wiseman's four factors into our own personalities.

If you read the above descriptions of the quintessential lucky person and thought, "Oh no, sounds like the opposite of who I am!" then don't worry: there's a lot we can do to gently shift any mindset. It starts with *not* assuming that you are doomed to have an unlucky mindset! Instead, notice how your perspective gently changes when you think instead, "It's such a good thing that I'm learning about this now. I'm pretty lucky to have the chance to make a change."

Avoid the temptation to relish your bad luck and make it a part of your identity. This tendency often comes from a fear of change and the unknown.

To increase openness, try meditating

Fortune favors the prepared mind. But it also favors the relaxed, flexible mind, or what Buddhists call a "beginner's mind." Nothing could be better for loosening and expanding our perceptions than meditating. Even if you think you hate meditating or can't see how it applies to creating more luck, take the idea of starting a meditation practice itself as your first exercise in being open and receptive: why not say yes to something new? Who knows where it might lead?

You don't need to sit on a cushion or burn incense. Simply close your eyes and sit or lie somewhere quiet and undisturbed. Anchor in the present moment by engaging with each of your senses. Notice sights, sounds, smells and so on. The important word here is *notice* – you are not judging these stimuli, or interpreting them, or deciding whether you like them or not. You're just noticing. You don't follow any one thread over another. You don't "try" to do anything in particular; you just sit and be.

Such an exercise widens your perception – not to mention it relaxes you! No, sitting down to contemplate nothing in particular in this way won't directly make you luckier, but it will loosen you up, and make possible a kind of creative and open-ended way of looking at the world. If you can practice just experiencing something without trying to grasp it or avoid it or tell a story about it, you're more likely to just perceive it for what it is. And that makes you more creative and a much better problem solver. When you're relaxed, you're more likely to say yes to things, follow your nose, and think out of the box.

In the spirit of pure and open-ended perception, you can also foster the trait of openness to new experiences by... well, trying new experiences. Agree to something without thinking too hard about it first. Like Steve Jobs, sign up for a class or new hobby that you only have the dimmest inclination towards. Don't analyze the inclination too much or judge it or yourself – just go with it.

To improve your intuition, build self-trust

Most people have pretty good intuition. The trouble is that they don't *trust* their intuition when it appears and speaks to them. Something pops up inside, and they think, "I should say something" or "I should look into that." And then they don't. Blame it on fear, but many of us constantly doubt our gut feelings and hunches, and end up second guessing ourselves. Instead, we trust the opinions of others or assume that we're only qualified to have an opinion if we do loads of research beforehand.

While it's great to be prudent and cautious at times, it can also mean that we are less spontaneous, less relaxed, and far less open to whatever happens. In other words, less lucky.

One great way to build more trust in your own in-built intuition is to develop confidence in yourself. With confidence, you value your own ideas and opinions, and learn to respect and acknowledge your own limits, desires and feelings about things. If you have a feeling that something isn't right and that you shouldn't pursue it, you trust that feeling and listen to it. Without confidence in yourself, however, you're more likely to say, "you're being silly, there's no reason to think that," and then discount your intuition.

Now, your intuition might not always be right. Often human beings make quick assumptions that, on second look, are nothing more than bias and guesswork. But that's OK – we are only interested in cultivating a lucky *mindset*. If our intuition happens to be right once in a while and we're lucky because of it, so much the better, but the main benefit is the change that happens inside us when we relax and ourselves to "go with the flow."

There are plenty of ways to develop confidence in your own perceptions and estimations:

- As counterintuitive as it sounds, create an ultra-confident alter-ego that is you, only the best possible version. Then, try to see the world through their eyes. For example, you've been asked to take on a brand new project at work at the drop of a hat. What would your alter-ego, who has complete faith in themselves, do?
- Develop greater emotional awareness. As often as you can remember, pause and ask yourself *what you're feeling* in each moment. Try to put words to inner sensations, sense them in your body, and notice how your actions influence these feelings. Just as with meditation, don't judge or interpret the emotions you notice. Try not to rush to fix or change anything. Just give emotions space to be what they are. The more you know what you feel, the more clearly you'll know what you want, and the more you'll be able to trust your impulses instead of doubting yourself.
- If self-doubt is a problem, learn to take other people's opinions with a pinch of salt. Don't allow the perspectives of others to drown out your own – and that includes cultural attitudes and

conventions, too. Get into the habit of tuning others out and asking yourself what *you* feel, want and think. Other people's views are important, but make sure you don't allow their criticism, interpretations or agendas to color your own intuition. Advice can be invaluable – but not always!
- Finally, occasionally spend time alone so you can get to know yourself. Use a journal to explore everything that makes you who you are. The better grasp you have on yourself as a unique person, the more anchored you'll be in your own appraisals, and the next time your intuition speaks, even if it's only a whisper, you'll feel confident and relaxed enough to trust where it's pointing.

To improve positive expectations, keep a gratitude journal

One study Wiseman did was to ask the self-proclaimed unlucky people to keep a luck journal:

"We asked that at the end of each day, they write down the most positive thing that happened or most positive thought they had that day. Or, in some cases, something negative that used to happen that no longer happens, or at very least some thought of gratitude."

You can imagine the results. The participants very quickly started to shift their perspective, and experience that positive and hopeful frame of mind more associated with lucky people. They reported being able to see more opportunities and good things in their lives – the very same lives they felt so negative about before writing in their journals.

Looking for the silver lining is like training your perspective to see the good in things. You learn not to make the same mistakes, and you don't dwell on them or beat yourself up over anything. Remembering the power of a self-fulfilling prophesy, use gratitude to inoculate yourself against further negativity and prime your brain to look for the positive. You shift your attention from what isn't working, what's wrong, and what's out of your control to what *is* working, what *is* really quite fortunate already, and what you can change. At the very least, you may have a sudden realization of just how lucky you actually already are but never quite noticed!

A gratitude journal has all these positive benefits (and Wiseman is not the only one to have discovered them), but it will also boost your mood more generally and bring you into a relaxed, receptive state of mind. Basically, it feels good. And we've seen that when you feel good, you tend to find that positively reflected back at you from the world in general.

A gratitude or luck journal can take many forms. Do what feels natural and don't overthink it. You could try simply listing five things that you enjoyed or are thankful for that day, no matter how small. You could make a point of writing down descriptions of the things that made you happy that day, or all the ways that you are already lucky. If you notice yourself complaining or feeling passive or hard done by, pause, become aware of your perspective, and see if you can challenge yourself to think of something a little more positive or at least open-ended.

As in Wiseman's study, all you may have some days is the recognition that a negative thing is no longer as bad as it once was. Bring some humor to it. If you break a leg, laugh it off and consider yourself lucky for not breaking the other one, too.

To transform bad luck into good luck, adopt a growth mindset

Carol Dweck was the first to coin the term "growth mindset" to describe the attitude that most accompanied genuine learning. She argued that when people believed that growth and learning were possible, their entire outlook changed. They take challenges, obstacles and failures in their stride and don't give up, but instead look for the upside, the lesson or the insight. Compare this to a fixed mindset, which sees character traits like intelligence (or, in our case, luck) as fixed and unchanging. If nothing can be done to improve, then why bother? In fact, with a fixed mindset challenges, obstacles and failures are all avoided – along with the growth they come with. Failures are taken personally, and the ego takes a dent.

As you can see, there are parallels between a serendipity or lucky mindset, an internal locus of control and a growth mindset. Unlucky people, on the other hand, all share the same cluster of attitudes that we can describe as an external locus of control or a fixed, unlucky mindset.

Importantly, people with a growth or fixed mindset respectively don't experience different levels of failure or success – their difference rests purely in their interpretation of those events. If you want to become better at reframing bad luck as good luck, a growth mindset could be just what you need.

One key way that the growth mindset manifests itself is in its attitude towards failure. We can imagine that failure is akin to bad luck or unfortunate changes in fortune for our purposes. Counterfactual thinking will definitely help you turn a negative perspective on its head, but when you're in the middle of some unfortunate experience, it can be hard to see things differently.

Try the technique of *accepting every bit of bad luck as though it is really a gift*. With a growth mindset, we can see failure and challenge and the best teachers of all. We can also use it to see that seemingly bad luck today is just the seed of better luck tomorrow. This isn't some feel-good positive thinking exercise – genuinely turn the event or situation over in your mind until you can find the hidden value. The thing is, lucky people tend to do this naturally. They have indomitable spirits that always seem to be assuming that the best is just around the corner.

If you genuinely can't see any good in an unlucky event, don't assume there isn't one. Just conclude that you can't see it yet, or that it's still busy unfolding. This often is exactly the case – how many times have you heard people retroactively describe their trials and dark times as really the greatest things to ever happen to them?

Could an unlucky event actually be necessary or useful down the line? Could it be teaching you something or laying the groundwork for something better? Sometimes, you can shift your perspective by literally just changing the words you use. Instead of calling something a problem, call it a challenge, or simply say it's "interesting"! If you like, laugh it all off and say you're *glad* that life always throws something new your way to keep you on your feet. If you find yourself complaining, practice tacking on the phrase, "How lucky I am to…" and complete your thought. It may feel silly, but notice just how radically your energy and focus change.

"I'm late, and this bus is stuck in traffic, and I'm sick to death of it…"

"How lucky I am to be late and stuck in traffic…" If you say this to yourself, the thought shines a light on all the ways it might, in fact, be lucky to be in your predicament. Why not? Pull out a book, have a little nap, or strike up a conversation with that interesting person a few seats over.

Takeaways

- Study findings shared in Wiseman's book *The Luck Factor* point to four factors that are responsible for a mindset most prone to luck. While these attitudes and traits don't literally cause luck in themselves, they do lay the groundwork and make us more able to capitalize on luck when it comes our way.
- The first factor is openness to new experiences, which means being aware and perceptive of lucky turns and emerging events in your environment, rather than shut out to novel possibilities. We can increase this factor in ourselves by practicing non-judgment and heightened awareness during meditation.
- The second factor is to listen to your gut and follow intuitions rather than getting bogged down in self-doubt, second guessing and analysis paralysis. We can improve this factor by building our self-

trust. By spending time alone to figure out your own thoughts rather than become overwhelmed by other people's, you can develop confidence in your own appraisals.
- The third factor is to harbor positive expectations, i.e., believing that good things will come. This will build the grit and resilience needed for luck to find you. This can be developed by creating a gratitude or luck journal, to shift your focus onto the positive and train your brain to expect good things.
- The fourth factor is the ability to reframe "bad" luck as good luck. Luckiness is a question of perception, and we can reinterpret seemingly unfortunate events by adopting a growth mindset. This will allow us to see the lesson in mistakes, employ counterfactual thinking and accept the hidden value in any outcome.
- With the above factors in place, we can not only *notice* luck around us more easily, but we can start to *create* the conditions for its unfolding.

Chapter 7. "Strategic Luck Planning"

Again, we are faced with the question: Is there a way to control and increase your luck? Is there a *strategy* to boost your chances of success? Let's try to pull all of the information we've explored into one solid strategy.

We know Richard Wiseman's stance — absolutely, there is a way to boost your luck, and he expands his four factors into eight (well, seven and a half) personality traits one can cultivate deliberately. Some of these were explored in the previous chapter.

However, according to Max Gunther, there are actually a whopping 13 types of mindset that are likely to lead to luck, fortune and serendipity. Gunther was an author and researcher who was best known for his controversial bestseller on financial risk management, *The Zurich Axioms,* but he also wrote other works, including *The Luck Factor*; *The Very, Very Rich;* and *Instant Millionaires.*

His book on *strategic luck planning* outlines 13 different techniques for discovering and taking advantage of life's good breaks. You'll notice that there's some overlap between his theory and Wiseman's – according to him, some people are born with good fortune, while others need a little more deliberate strategy to get what they desire. If you're reading this book, chances are you fall into the latter category. Either way, these 13 steps will help you do whatever you can to put you on the luckiest path forward.

How do the lucky organize their lives? Let's take a look:

Luck vs. Planning

The first of Gunther's rules is that luck and planning are two separate things that should never be confused. When a desired outcome is brought about by luck, you must acknowledge that fact. However, luck is not involved if you take the time to plan for the unexpected and things end up going well.

You need to have a crystal clear understanding of the role of cause and effect in your life, as well as know how to delineate what is pure chance or random unknown variables. If you end up confusing luck with planning, you all but guarantee that your luck will turn bad in the long run. Planning for something and then thinking it was just luck would take away the importance of all the planning that you have put in, and in the future, you may not repeat what caused your success. Being lucky and thinking that it was your planning that caused it will give you a distorted idea of what actually works, setting you up for failure later on when your luck runs out.

We live in a complex and unpredictable world. The first step for improving your luck is to recognize that it exists, but that you aren't successful *only* because of it. Our locus of control can impact our interpretation of good and bad events; unlucky people tend to blame bad luck when they fail and their own hard work when they succeed. But though this may feel good in the short term, it disempowers you.

Be humble when you win, and don't be too hard on yourself when you lose. After all, without the occasional loss, there would be no reason to improve. Try to take ego out of the picture entirely and simply become curious about what is happening. Learn from your mistakes, observe what unfolded, what could have been done better, and how external factors affected the outcome. If planning was why you were successful, then do it again. If it was luck, then find a way to ensure planning would have the same effect.

Likewise, don't take advice from people who got lucky about how to earn success through hard work – they simply don't know! Likewise, don't discredit the good actions of yourself or others simply because the results have been disproportionately unlucky. Realize when people are taking credit where they shouldn't, and be realistic about being sold big cheesy narratives that ultra-successful people would like you to believe.

This attitude makes a huge difference to your ability to learn, adapt and evolve. Take responsibility for your fate and pay attention to the results you're getting. The person who knows the difference between luck and planning will always win out over the person with raw luck who nevertheless misunderstands their fortune. Whatever you do, don't shrug and assume you can't gain insight into the mechanisms behind the outcome, or that you have no control over them. After something goes your way, just ask – how much of this was luck, and how much planning? Be as honest as you can.

Find the Fast Flow

Have you ever thought to yourself that nothing ever happens to you? That events and opportunities just pass you by? This may be because you don't position yourself in the best situations. Even if you are a quiet person, all you need to do is go to where the events flow fastest. Surround yourself with a churning mass of people, and things will inevitably happen. The more complex and well-connected a network you can insert yourself into, the more channels you create for luck to come and find you. All you need is to meet a lot of people and let them know who you are. The rest will come naturally, and they will direct opportunities your way.

There is no use sitting around waiting for things to just fall in your lap. Reclusive or aloof people are not lucky and have to grind through life on hard work alone. Instead, go where things are happening. Keep abreast of current events. Be curious, put your best foot forward, be interested in people, and make conversation. When you meet someone, ask about their life, their goals, their passions. Some of the most interesting people you will ever meet could be right in front of you, if only you had the initiative to look.

The more activity churning around you, the more luck will be included. This doesn't happen if you confine yourself to your room each night. You can't court luck directly, but you can build rapport with the people around you, be sociable and friendly, make contact, charm others, and generally, make sure that you're not on the sidelines of life but an active player. Make sure that you are on people's minds, or they'll forget about you, and nothing will get sent your way. In the context of luck, isolation really is a dead-end.

Take Calculated Risks

There are two ways to guarantee unsuccessfulness.

One is to take risks that are out of proportion to the rewards being sought. For example, putting all your money toward an investment that you haven't properly researched is a recipe for disaster, because even though the reward might be large, the chances of failure outweigh this reward.

The other way to ensure a lack of success and a lack of luck is to not take any risks at all, even when a perfect opportunity presents itself, like not wanting to talk to someone attractive even though you have been assured by three separate people that they like you. Think of it as extreme risk-aversion.

Lucky people avoid both extremes.

Unlucky people tend to let fear or over analysis undermine them and pull them out of the flow of the moment. This usually means they end up hesitating when they need to take a risk, or occasionally acting on misguided impulse and going too far to the other extreme – and then regretting it. You need to play to win, but that doesn't mean you have to gamble recklessly. Rather, commit to sticking your neck out in a *calculated* way.

Good luck is all about getting a favorable outcome from an uncertain situation. The best way to do this is to take measured risks that are supported by the evidence and data, anticipating the possible disasters and knowing how to deal with them. But don't get trapped in analyzing mode – at some point, you have to just act and be willing to face the consequences, good or bad.

To truly succeed, you need to understand the difference between foolish and calculated risks and know that some risk-taking is infinitely better than none at all. You can't sit on the sidelines and expect to be successful, but you can't leap at every opportunity that is shiny. No risk is as bad as excessive risk. You must walk a thin line which can only be ascertained through experience, practice, and failure. Don't merely copy the risks other people have taken – do your own research and have faith in your own assessments. At the very least, understand that failing after taking a risk is not really the end of the world (there's that growth mindset again!).

Cut Your Losses

This point is all about something that affects us all: greed.

Say you're on a lucky streak and things just keep going your way. We have the tendency to believe that this will continue, but unfortunately, this will never be the case. You can call this arrogance, the Gambler's Fallacy, or a simple lack of foresight. You've probably heard the expression "don't push your luck" and there's wisdom in that – if you know when to call it a day.

Knowing when to cut your losses and walk away is an important part of the road to success. You need to always assume that a run of luck is going to be short and never try to ride a run to its peak. Your "optimal stopping point" is often a little earlier than you would like! With this kind of thinking, the law of averages is heavily on your side, and you will be more likely to succeed if you accept that based on probability, your luck *will* eventually run out. As we saw in the first point about luck vs. planning, you'll be in trouble if you don't even realize you're on a lucky run and simply assume that your hard work is the cause of your success – you'll be in for a nasty surprise!

Don't delude yourself into thinking that something good will last forever, or that you have it all figured out. You will end up losing everything before you know it – especially if you haven't done anything to gain insight or understanding into why you've been successful. Imagine a person who has been lucky in life to have a string of romantic partners that are "catches." Not realizing this lucky streak for what it is, such a person may be less hesitant to break up and move on, in the expectation they can do even better. But once this lucky streak runs out, the person realizes the role that luck was in fact playing all along, and how difficult it will be to find another amazing person. They're like the gambler who confidently let their bet ride, only to lose everything.

It may be hard to accept that there was a chance that you could have "won" something more, but it will always be harder to accept that you ended up losing it all. You might be lucky, but you won't be lucky forever. If you throw a coin a thousand times, chances are you'll get at least one "long run" where the same side comes up 9 times in a row. This is just a statistical and probabilistic feature. But in 1000 throws you will also come up with many more "short runs" of four in a row. If you roll three in a row, how do you know if you're in a short turn or a long one? You don't!

We tend to hear the stories of people who made it by pushing a run, and then luckily finding out that this risk paid off. But we seldom hear about those people that did well by making the best of short runs, which are more plentiful anyway. You have more to gain cumulatively by not pushing your luck on small runs of luck than you do to lose if you gamble everything on the off chance that you're in a long run. Sure, life is not exactly like a casino game, but many of the same principles apply. Quit while you're ahead. Appreciate and enjoy a lucky streak, but don't *depend* on it. Certainly don't expect it to last forever.

Select Your Luck

This is a carryover from the last point. So, we know that if your luck is good, stick with it and enjoy it as much as you can. But what if your luck is bad?

It is important to realize that some opportunities will never lead to great things. All investments, whether they be time, money, or love, will encounter problems. What you need to ask yourself is whether there is a likelihood that these problems will go away. Do you have some realistic hope of fixing them? If so, then stay aboard. If not, then you should get out and look for better luck elsewhere. In a sense, selecting your luck means knowing where good luck will flow, as well as knowing when to withdraw from a hopeless cause and spend your energy elsewhere.

Sometimes we can be so sure of an idea, whether it's a career, relationship, business investment, or something else. Perhaps you landed a job that seemed thrilling to you and eventually you realized there was no hope of progression in that position. Perhaps it's a new relationship that's quickly lost its sheen. Sometimes what seemed like a great idea in the beginning doesn't always work out when implemented – and that's OK! But succumbing to the "sunk cost fallacy" and sticking with situations we know will not have a good outcome can seriously erode our luck, for obvious reasons.

The trouble can come when we're unwilling to admit that we were wrong and instead stubbornly cling to an idea that has long since outlived its usefulness.. People can struggle to change their paths because it means that they weren't unlucky; the misfortune was down to them and them alone. But making mistakes is inevitable, and not necessarily something that will derail your plans – unless you let them. What's worse than taking a wrong turn is staying on that wrong path, with no hope of survival, getting further and further from where you want to be.

Here, lucky people differ from unlucky ones in that they can be *more* pessimistic when they need to be. It takes a certain kind of cold realism to acknowledge that a certain course has no future, and then quickly cut ties before it's too late. But people who do this free themselves up for better choices and opportunities immediately afterwards. They don't get trapped throwing time, money, energy or hopes down a black hole that will never give them anything back.

Take the Zig-Zag Path

Despite what many people think (and what many of us are actively told), the path to success is rarely a straight line.

Even the most well-thought-out plan doesn't always work, and keeping to the same path may lead you nowhere. As we've seen, lucky people do not have trouble deviating from their course. It's not that they intend to deviate, but they are simply open to the deviation and seize opportunity when it comes because it might be a better path overall. They do not have a misplaced sense of loyalty to the path they're already on, and have no qualms about not having a neat, pretty narrative of how they got from A to B.

Plans work best when they are used as a guide, and if something better comes along, the plan should be discarded immediately and without regret. It's not uncommon to have a set goal in mind, perhaps a career that you have always dreamt of, and begin to realize the job you have might not be the best to get you there.

When guiding a 4x4 on sandy terrain, drivers are told to loosen their grip on the steering wheel and resist steering against the minor turns to the left and right the car makes as it winds through ripples and bumps in the sand. Instead, they're told to keep the car in roughly the right direction, but to try not to correct any side-to-side movement, or risk getting stuck. Life can be a little like that – we don't need to white-knuckle our way through things. Instead, we can see what's working, and follow that without too much forceful control. Ultimately, this gets us where we need to go more quickly and with less effort.

Change can be difficult, but sometimes, it can lead to the best outcome. Try a different job, accept opportunities with arms wide open, exploit a newly discovered talent, take advantage of serendipity, and if these things don't work out, then find something else. Relax your grip a little on how you achieve the outcome.

It's impossible to predict what will happen in the future, so don't take long-term plans seriously. They can act as a guide, but unforeseen opportunities are the ones that will really get you places. Nobody has ever had an easy path to success, and you should always be prepared and willing to veer off your chosen course. The zig-zag path, in hindsight, looks incredibly lucky and fortuitous when in reality, you were just okay with discarding plans and taking risks.

Supernatural Belief

Gunther refers to supernaturalism as any belief in an unseen spirit, force, or agency whose existence has not been proved to anyone's satisfaction. But how can this belief help you? It's not because it makes you luckier, but because it helps you make impossible choices. Sometimes there is no rational choice to make, but the worse reaction is to do nothing.

A supernatural belief can help people get into a potentially winning position by helping them make choices. For example, lucky numbers and omens may not be proven, but they can help you take a quick leap of faith into a decision that you may not have been able to make otherwise.

Use superstition and be irrational when things are in your favor, and be rational when they aren't. Who cares if the planets truly did align or if it was just in your mind, as long as it gives you the confidence to take action? This is related to taking a zig-zag path in that deviating from what is planned or conventional, or even realistic, is sometimes the best course of action for luck.

Be A Bit Pessimistic

According to this theory, lucky people, as a breed, tend to be more pessimistic than unlucky people – if we are careful with how we define pessimism. Optimism means expecting the best, but good luck involves knowing how you'll handle the worst. As discussed earlier, good luck often means taking risks, but it doesn't mean being foolish about it. To avoid bad luck, you need to know how to handle the worst-case scenario. And you can only do that if you've actually considered what that scenario is. Lucky people, therefore, don't necessarily see a glass as half-empty, but they do think about how to handle it if it were indeed half-empty. In essence, lucky people hope for the best but are prepared for the worst.

Think about what is the worst that could happen in any situation, and then come up with a solution to protect yourself from these outcomes.

Written agreements, budget plans, or getting insurance are examples of how you have to protect yourself from the worst. Lucky people plan ahead and are accountable. They take action to protect themselves and then don't dwell on it. They cross their t's and dot their i's to set themselves up for luck and success as best they can. But make sure you don't let your pessimism keep you from trying or cause you to give up. Use your pessimism to your advantage, but don't let it hold you back.

Shut Up

When given the opportunity, we can often talk ourselves into a variety of situations that are not what we want. Talk can tie you up and lock you into positions that may seem right today but may be wrong tomorrow. When there is no good reason to say something, say nothing. Any opinion has the ability to polarize people, and you never know whom you are going to polarize.

Lucky people are careful of what they say and to whom they say it. They don't take strong positions on controversial topics if they can avoid it. Talk has a way of spreading like wildfire, especially if it wasn't the intention. Too much talk can constrict your choices, and you may find yourself in a situation where you think, "Why did I agree to this?" Remember that finding new plans and taking random opportunities are the keys to success, and you can't do this if you've talked yourself into something that you can't get out of. Mind your tongue because it can pigeon-hole you or even burn bridges before you know it. On the other hand, being a neutral presence as a default can work in your favor.

Recognize a Non-Lesson

A non-lesson is an experience in life that seems to be a lesson but actually isn't. Not everything means something or implies something. You need to recognize when something was just bad luck and move on. In fact, it may not have even been bad luck — it was just a random event that you can't make any conclusions from. You can't learn anything about how to get better luck here, either.

Do not generalize or create theories out of random events, or it will just lead to you avoid things you have no reason to avoid. If you have several bad dating experiences, it doesn't mean all men or women are impossible to date. It only means you have had a few bad experiences and need to improve how you choose people.

Knowing that human beings tend to construct meaning where they don't find any, and seek patterns to help manage the appearance of randomness, commit to being comfortable with the fact that sometimes bad things just happen. You could construct an elaborate story about how your car accident was really a special lesson sent to you by the gods to teach you a life lesson about... whatever. It might be true, but how would you know? And more importantly, does having that belief actually enrich your life? You may find more relief, healing and meaning in acknowledging that sometimes road accidents happen, and that's that.

By following non-lessons, you risk missing out on many good things in life just because of bad luck or a few bad experiences. You also risk creating personal myths and narratives to help explain something that truthfully doesn't have much of an explanation, and these personal myths and narratives can be limiting or flat-out wrong. Be wary of these fallacies, and don't let them guide your decisions. This is tough because we are powerfully conditioned to seek pleasure and avoid pain, so it requires getting past that instinct and removing the fear from anything negative you've experienced.

Accept that the Universe is Unfair

Related to this point, all of us, even the most optimistic, have had the occasional thought that the universe is out to get us. Although this may be counterproductive in some cases, it is important to accept that life is hard, and, most times, unfair. All of us — the good, the bad, and the in-between — are equally as likely to achieve our greatest dreams or live through our worst nightmares. You might be unlucky a few times in a row, and there will be nothing to make up for that fact. In other words, though we might want there to be meaning, or justice, or a logical cause and effect, sometimes there just isn't.

Kids get terminal diseases, people who don't try can end up succeeding, good people will be unlucky, and bad people will have good luck. What matters is what you do with this piece of information.

Fairy tale happy endings are just not the norm in life, and you should never *expect* good things to happen because you deserve it. The universe, evidently, does not run on "deserve." You don't deserve good luck, and you shouldn't expect a break. We will all experience bad luck regardless of our hard work or good intentions because of how little is actually in our control. The important thing is to accept that everyone has it hard and probably sometimes thinks the universe is against them, as well. Accepting that things will always be unfair will prevent you from anger, self-torture, or giving up. It will also, ironically, make you appreciate all the wonderful things you *do* have, and how they were never a given. If you can truly grasp and accept unfairness, you are in a sense liberated – you do not wait around for what you want to happen. You make it happen.

Be Willing to Be Busy

Have you ever noticed that people with the most opportunities are those who seem to be the busiest? This is because the more activities you have going on, the greater the likelihood that an opening could present itself. Juggle as many ventures as you can, take up new hobbies, join new classes. One of them could be the gateway to your lucky break.

Avoid idleness. This will lead you nowhere. How can you expect to succeed if you wait for the opportunities to come to you when you can just as easily go out and search for them yourself? Follow your curiosity and let it guide you. Engage in projects you like and keep trying until you get your lucky break. Remember, in Gunther's view, luck clearly is not a blessing sent from above; it's the product of hard work and time spent. If you're busy, eventually, you'll run into something that you'd deem lucky.

Find A Destiny Partner

A destiny partner is someone who changes your luck over a period of time.

This is not necessarily a romantic partner and is usually someone just found by blind luck, though it can help if you are actively looking. Maybe it's someone you talk your ideas through that inspires you to do better things. Maybe it's someone who always seems to lead good opportunities your way. There are people who can change the course of your life and the nature of your luck, and you can often do the same to them. Destiny pairs can cause an explosion of good luck when they work together.

Some people are just naturally average by themselves, able to achieve, but struggling to do so. Sometimes, all it takes to become incredible is the company of the right partner. This person can be a spouse, business partner, colleague, or friend. Meeting them happens by chance, so pay attention to your gut. Your destiny pair will elicit a quick, strong, and positive reaction, and good things will begin to unfurl.

Each of Gunther's 13 steps has the potential to change your life, if you genuinely work to put them into practice. A lot of the time, luck is out of your hands, but with these strategic planning techniques, you have the ability to control as much as you can – which may be a lot more than you first thought. Whether you agree more with Wiseman's approach to luck or feel that Gunther has a better theory, one thing remains clear: it is your attitude and your willingness to achieve that is the sole difference between waiting for life to give you what you desire or going out there and hunting down success on your own.

Takeaways:

- According to author Max Gunther, there are 13 attitudes, traits and habits that set lucky people apart from unlucky ones. Lucky people clearly understand the difference between luck and planning, and never confuse them. They repeat hard work that gets results, and are grateful for luck when it happens, knowing they weren't responsible.
- Lucky people find the "fast flow" of people and information and position themselves within it, being extroverted and sociable and building connections with others to maximize possible channels for luck. Lucky people take appropriate risks – neither overextending themselves nor

being too hesitant. They allow data and research to guide them.
- When something isn't working, know when to cut your losses and move on. Quit while you're ahead rather than risk losing it all on a bet that your luck will continue. On a related note, "select" your luck by cutting ties with any course that is 100% not going anywhere, rather than wasting more time and effort on it.
- The path to success is usually a zig-zag and not a straight line, so relax and become curious about the most optimal – even if unexpected – path from A to B. Superstitions can help you make decisions in impossible situations, since they encourage you to act rather than freeze with indecisiveness. A little irrationality won't hurt if it ultimately gets you to do the right thing!
- Pessimism can be a useful thing if it helps you to protect yourself and plan for when things go well. Lucky people plan for the worst but expect the best. Gunther also believes that lucky people don't narrow their possibilities by talking indiscriminately about controversial or divisive topics – it makes sense if you're trying to connect optimally with people!

- Recognize a "non-lesson" which is just bad luck but doesn't mean anything. Don't twist yourself in knots trying to understand it. Likewise, accept that you are owed nothing and that none of us "deserves" luck or a charmed life.
- Avoid idleness and stay busy to increase your exposure to lucky new opportunities. Finally, partner up with people that seem to improve your luck, or pass opportunities your way.

Summary Guide

INTRODUCTION

- Luck may play a bigger role in our success than we think. By examining what we consider lucky breaks, serendipity and fortuitous events, we can better handle the invisible forces that favor some and not others.
- Research has made surprising findings, i.e., that it may be better to be mediocre in skills but lucky than to be highly talented yet unlucky. Mathematical models have tended to show the irrelevance of skill and talent, and emphasize the fact that randomness plays a big part in what we consider success.
- In the case of the discovery of LSD (and many other scientific advances), we can see that luck plays a surprising role.
- Luck may play a role in an absolute sense in determining the hand we're dealt in what Warren Buffett calls the "Ovarian Lottery" – where we're born, our genes, and so on. But hard work does matter,

and may factor in a more relative sense, i.e., it helps us distinguish ourselves from others who have been similarly lucky.
- Luck and hard work play a part. We cannot control luck, but we can understand how it works and position ourselves accordingly, so that we're ready to strike when and if opportunity does come our way.

CHAPTER 1. LUCK OF THE DRAW

- Humans have an innate need to live in a world that makes sense to them, and which they feel they can control and influence. We want to predict, model and manage the world, but this combined with our tendency to find patterns where there are none, can make our *perceptions* of probability very different from the reality.
- The way we experience and explain random events, and the cause to which we attribute these events, is highly personal. We may have an internal or external locus of control, which is whether we believe we are the cause of life's events (the former) or whether our lives are at the mercy of external events beyond our control (the latter).

- Research has discovered that there are further distinctions, and that an external locus of control can see luck as either a stable quality a person possesses, or a fleeting phenomenon that could disappear as quickly as it comes. The finding is that viewing luck as stable makes people more proactive – and more successful.
- Attribution theory deals with how we attach meaning to our own behavior and the behavior of other people. How we assign blame and praise depends on how we understand accountability and our influence on events – and it has a powerful influence on how likely we are to act and actually achieve success.

CHAPTER 2. WHAT TO BELIEVE

- There are two popular ideas worth exploring when it comes to the concept of luck: the law of attraction, and the idea of a self-fulfilling prophesy. Research into the effectiveness of the law of attraction (or wishful thinking) yields no support, and indicates that fantasy can actually undermine success by making us less likely to take useful action.

- A self-fulfilling prophecy is a prediction that directly or indirectly *causes itself* to become true due to positive feedback between belief and behavior. It proves how powerful belief can be.
- If you believe you are a lucky person, you are more likely to create that reality yourself — not out of thin air, or by magic, but because you are proactively taking steps to make that outcome a reality.
- Robert Wiseman and Alan Kirman have independently discovered that being lucky may come down to believing that you are lucky.
- Lucky people do visualize, yet they tend to imagine not the outcome but the performance of the practical steps needed to reach that outcome. They tend to be positive and optimistic, easily forget past mistakes, trust their gut feelings, and put a positive interpretation on events by imagining how things could have been so much worse. This, in effect, means that people who believe they're lucky, are!

CHAPTER 3. WHAT TO THINK

- Seneca famously said, "luck is where preparation meets opportunity." There is plenty we can do to prepare ourselves so that we are ready to notice and seize new opportunities that emerge, and make ourselves more "lucky."
- There are three main traits associated with being a lucky person. The first is extroversion, which leads us to engage with others socially, speak out, make connections and win others over. This will naturally create more opportunities for help, random connections, or new information that can spell a lucky break.
- The second trait is open-mindedness, which is a receptive, spontaneous state of mind that approaches life with curiosity rather than fear, bias or expectation. With openness to new experiences, we say yes to new opportunities and encounter more life experiences that have the chance to evolve favorably.
- The third trait is low neuroticism. When we are relaxed and not acting from fear, we see solutions, think outside the box and encounter unexpected positive outcomes – and we don't jeopardize any good luck we do encounter!
- There are three thought patterns associated with being lucky. Believing in

karma means you take your actions seriously and are more likely to have a proactive internal locus of control, and treat others well – naturally leading to more luck opportunities.
- Belief in your own competence and ability to withstand adversity creates resilience, meaning you take beneficial action for longer, which means you increase your chances of a positive outcome.
- Finally, lucky people learn what works and deliberately try to recreate those conditions that they know have led to luck for them in the past.

CHAPTER 4. WHAT TO DO

- Our luck comes in part from our behaviors and choices, and those in turn come from our mindset and the way we think.
- If luck = preparation + opportunity, and we cannot control what opportunities come our way, then it means the only way to improve our luck is to focus on being prepared to strike when a lucky chance does come our way.

- An obvious way to bring more luck to your life is to work hard, even if the results are far off or not guaranteed.
- Hard work isn't all that matters, though. The surface area theory of luck explains that our luck is a result of both *doing* and *telling*, i.e., hard work combined with how ready we are to talk about our passion with others. You can construct your own doing/telling graph to determine where you need to put your efforts to increase your luck.
- We can also increase luck by using the methods of visualization and positive affirmations. Both have been shown scientifically to improve performance and lead to better outcomes. To work well, visualizations have to be rich and vivid, and affirmations have to be said regularly. Naturally, both work best when paired with concrete action taken towards your goals!
- Superstitious behaviors are a human tendency that evolved in the face of uncertainty, as a way to feel in control. There is no magic, but belief in the power of a superstition can be powerful in itself. The best superstitions, however, are those that encourage an internal locus of control

and which don't distort our perception of what is and isn't under our control.

CHAPTER 5. COINCIDENCE AND SERENDIPITY

- Coincidence and serendipity are related to good luck. We all would like something beneficial and fortuitous to happen to us for seemingly no good reason. We can't create positive random chances, but we can foster a "serendipity mindset" that helps us notice and take advantage of the chances that come our way.
- Serendipity means different things to different people, but generally, it is the combination of seemingly improbable occurrences plus positive personal feelings about them. We can cultivate a serendipity mindset by recognizing triggers in daily life, drawing connections to other unrelated areas, and finding potential value in that link.
- Making use of the unexpected requires that we are optimistic, open-ended, comfortable with ambiguity, extraverted, and good listeners, as well as willing to make mistakes or entertain unexpected outcomes. We need to be proactive and

curious about what emerges spontaneously.
- The real difference between the status quo and serendipity is in the effort you put in following a chance happening, and the meaning you can assign to events after the fact.
- Statistician David Hand claims that although coincidences seem surprising, "extremely improbable events are commonplace." It is only the limits of our human understanding of probability that makes coincidence seem more astonishing.
- Luck is a way of describing our interaction with random external events. Those who are religious or spiritual tend to experience more coincidences and perceive them differently. Similarly, self-referential people – i.e., those who tend to connect external events to themselves – also describe more coincidence experiences.

CHAPTER 6. WISEMAN'S FOUR FACTORS

- Study findings shared in Wiseman's book *The Luck Factor* point to four factors that are responsible for a mindset most prone to luck. While these attitudes and traits don't literally cause luck in themselves, they do lay the groundwork and make us more able to capitalize on luck when it comes our way.
- The first factor is openness to new experiences, which means being aware and perceptive of lucky turns and emerging events in your environment, rather than shut out to novel possibilities. We can increase this factor in ourselves by practicing non-judgment and heightened awareness during meditation.
- The second factor is to listen to your gut and follow intuitions rather than getting bogged down in self-doubt, second guessing and analysis paralysis. We can improve this factor by building our self-trust. By spending time alone to figure out your own thoughts rather than become overwhelmed by other people's, you can develop confidence in your own appraisals.

- The third factor is to harbor positive expectations, i.e., believing that good things will come. This will build the grit and resilience needed for luck to find you. This can be developed by creating a gratitude or luck journal, to shift your focus onto the positive and train your brain to expect good things.
- The fourth factor is the ability to reframe "bad" luck as good luck. Luckiness is a question of perception, and we can reinterpret seemingly unfortunate events by adopting a growth mindset. This will allow us to see the lesson in mistakes, employ counterfactual thinking and accept the hidden value in any outcome.
- With the above factors in place, we can not only *notice* luck around us more easily, but we can start to *create* the conditions for its unfolding.

CHAPTER 7. "STRATEGIC LUCK PLANNING"

- According to author Max Gunther, there are 13 attitudes, traits and habits that set lucky people apart from unlucky ones. Lucky people clearly understand the difference between luck and planning, and

never confuse them. They repeat hard work that gets results, and are grateful for luck when it happens, knowing they weren't responsible.
- Lucky people find the "fast flow" of people and information and position themselves within it, being extroverted and sociable and building connections with others to maximize possible channels for luck. Lucky people take appropriate risks – neither overextending themselves nor being too hesitant. They allow data and research to guide them.
- When something isn't working, know when to cut your losses and move on. Quit while you're ahead rather than risk losing it all on a bet that your luck will continue. On a related note, "select" your luck by cutting ties with any course that is 100% not going anywhere, rather than wasting more time and effort on it.
- The path to success is usually a zig-zag and not a straight line, so relax and become curious about the most optimal – even if unexpected – path from A to B. Superstitions can help you make decisions in impossible situations, since they encourage you to act rather than freeze with indecisiveness. A little irrationality

won't hurt if it ultimately gets you to do the right thing!
- Pessimism can be a useful thing if it helps you to protect yourself and plan for when things go well. Lucky people plan for the worst but expect the best. Gunther also believes that lucky people don't narrow their possibilities by talking indiscriminately about controversial or divisive topics – it makes sense if you're trying to connect optimally with people!
- Recognize a "non-lesson" which is just bad luck but doesn't mean anything. Don't twist yourself in knots trying to understand it. Likewise, accept that you are owed nothing and that none of us "deserves" luck or a charmed life.
- Avoid idleness and stay busy to increase your exposure to lucky new opportunities. Finally, partner up with people that seem to improve your luck, or pass opportunities your way.

www.ingramcontent.com/pod-product-compliance
Lightning Source LLC
Chambersburg PA
CBHW020525080526
44583CB00013B/737